Great Walks on the
ENGLAND
COAST PATH

30 classic walks on the longest National Trail

by Andrew McCloy

CICERONE

Printed in China on behalf of Latitude Press Ltd
A catalogue record for this book is available from the British Library.
All photographs are by the author unless otherwise stated.

Updates to this guide

While every effort is made by our authors to ensure the accuracy of guidebooks as they go to print, changes can occur during the lifetime of an edition. Any updates that we know of for this guide will be on the Cicerone website (www.cicerone.co.uk/989/updates), so please check before planning your trip. We also advise that you check information about such things as transport, accommodation and shops locally. Even rights of way can be altered over time. We are always grateful for information about any discrepancies between a guidebook and the facts on the ground, sent by email to updates@cicerone.co.uk or by post to Cicerone, Juniper House, Murley Moss, Oxenholme Road, Kendal, LA9 7RL.

Register your book: To sign up to receive free updates, special offers and GPX files where available, register your book in your Cicerone library at www.cicerone.co.uk.

Acknowledgements

Many people helped with the research, walking and checking of this book, but in particular thanks to Ange Harker and Ben Nichols of Natural England, Wirral Council, Tony Lamberton and Friends of Hilbre, Mark Owen and the South West Coast Path Association, Judi Darley of Chichester Harbour Conservancy, Yorkshire Wildlife Trust, Durham Heritage Coast partnership, Fiona Barltrop, Vivienne Crow, Chiz Dakin, Russell Wheeler and last, but certainly not least, Penny and Caitlin McCloy for sharing this epic coastal adventure.

Front cover: The beach at Bamburgh castle (Walk 30) (photo: Madeline Williams)
Page 1: Dunes on the Sefton coast (Walk 5)
Page 2-3: The River Stiffkey near Morston (Walk 25)

Contents

Route symbols on OS map extracts
(for OS legend see printed OS maps)

~~~ route

~~~ alternative route

~~~ extension

(SF) start/finish point

(S) start point

(F) finish point

➤ route direction

SCALE: 1:50,000

0 kilometres 0.5 1

0 miles 0.5

Features on the overview map

——— County/Unitary boundary

——— National boundary

Urban area

National Park
eg **BRECON BEACONS**

Forest Park/National Forest
eg *National Forest*

Area of Outstanding Natural
Beauty/National Scenic Area
eg *Dedham Vale*

400m
200m
75m
0m

GPX files for all routes can be downloaded free at www.cicerone.co.uk/989/GPX.

Top: Branscombe beach and cliffs (Walk 15) (photo: Chiz Dakin)
Middle: Morecambe Bay from Arnside Knott (Walk 3) (photo: Chiz Dakin)
Bottom: Morecambe Bay from Arnside Point (Walk 3)

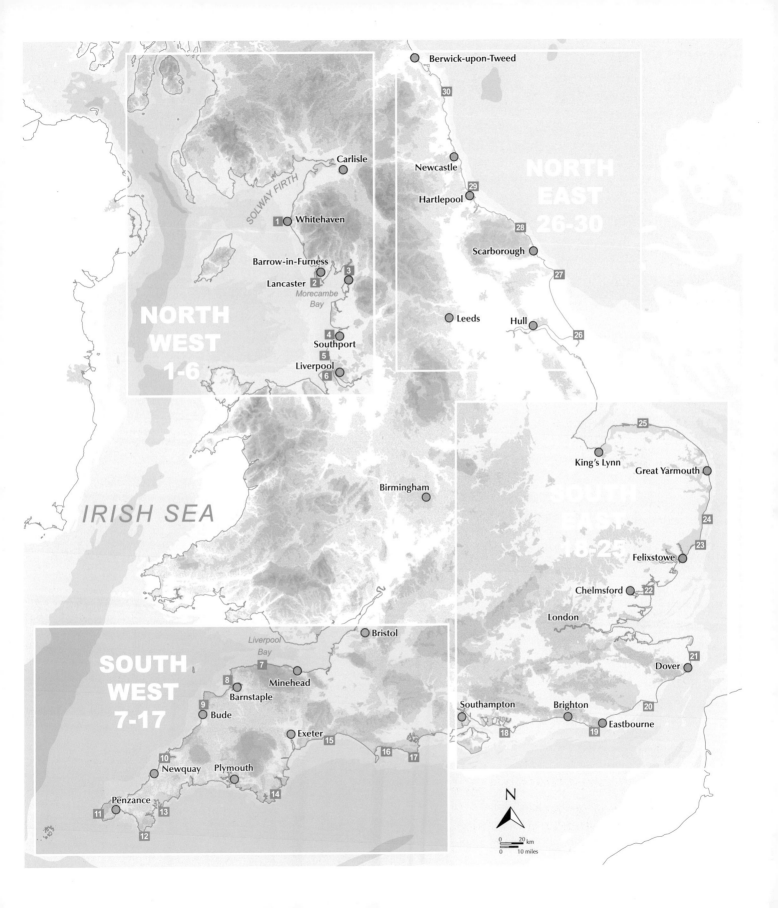

Route summary table

No	Start	Finish	Distance	Ascent	Time	Page
North West						
1	Whitehaven	St Bees	10.5km (6.5 miles)	505m (1660ft)	3hr 30min	29
2	Walney Island	Walney Island	26km (16 miles)	180m (590ft)	6hr	34
3	Arnside	Arnside	9km (5.6 miles)	260m (850ft)	2hr 45min	41
4	Lancaster	Cockerham	18.75km (11.6 miles)	40m (130ft)	4hr 15min	45
5	Southport	Crosby	31km (19.2 miles)	60m (200ft)	8hr	51
6	New Brighton	Heswall	25km (15.5 miles)	100m (330ft)	5hr 30min	57
South West						
7	Lynton	Combe Martin	21km (13 miles)	1305m (4280ft)	7hr	67
8	Woolacombe	Woolacombe	14.5km (9 miles)	335m (1100ft)	3hr 30min	72
9	Hartland Quay	Bude	23.5km (14.6 miles)	1335m (4380ft)	8hr	78
10	Padstow	Porthcothan	21.25km (13.2 miles)	575m (1890ft)	5hr 30min	85
11	Pendeen	Penzance	45.5km (28.3 miles)	1100m (3610ft)	13hr	90
12	Lizard	Lizard	14km (8.7 miles)	330m (1080ft)	3hr 30min	97
13	Portscatho	Portscatho	15.75km (9.8 miles)	290m (950ft)	4hr	102
14	Beesands	Beesands	23km (14.3 miles)	650m (2130ft)	6hr	107
15	Beer	Beer	9.75km (6 miles)	405m (1330ft)	3hr	112
16	Lulworth Cove	Lulworth Cove	13.75km (8.5 miles)	505m (1660ft)	3hr 30min	116
17	Worth Matravers	Worth Matravers	12km (7.5 miles)	370m (1210ft)	3hr	121
South East						
18	Bosham Quay	Bosham Quay	16.5km (10.2 miles)	10m (30ft)	5hr	129
19	Seaford	Eastbourne	21km (13 miles)	640m (2100ft)	5hr 30min	134
20	Dungeness	Dungeness	14km (8.7 miles)	10m (30ft)	3hr 30min	140
21	Deal	Dover	15.5km (9.6 miles)	500m (1640ft)	4hr	144
22	Tollesbury	Tollesbury	15km (9.3 miles)	70m (230ft)	3hr 30min	151
23	Orford	Orford	10.25km (6.4 miles)	50m (170ft)	3hr	157
24	Walberswick	Walberswick	18km (11 miles)	140m (460ft)	4hr 30min	162
25	Burnham Deepdale	Sheringham	49.5km (30.7 miles)	85m (290ft)	11hr	168
North East						
26	Kilnsea	Kilnsea	13.25km (8.2 miles)	10m (30ft)	3hr 30min	177
27	Bridlington	Bempton	19km (11.8 miles)	595m (1950ft)	4hr 15min	182
28	Scarborough	Staithes	50.5km (31.4 miles)	2025m (6640ft)	12hr	188
29	Seaham	Hartlepool	26km (16 miles)	545m (1790ft)	6hr 30min	195
30	Craster	Bamburgh	22km (13.7 miles)	110m (360ft)	5hr	203

The Jurassic Coast around Lulworth (photo: Chiz Dakin) ▶

Introduction

Morecambe Bay from Blackstone Point (Walk 3)

How would you like to go for a long walk by the sea? Make that a very, very long walk – say, about 4500km or 2800 miles. That's the length, give or take a few steps, of the new walking trail around the entire coast of England. It means that every time you set off on one of the routes in this book, you will be walking a little bit of the longest coastal trail in the world!

As an island nation, the coast is in our DNA. Nowhere on the English mainland are you any more than 113km or 70 miles from the sea. We are, as author Patrick Barkham nicely puts it, 'more edge than middle'. England's relationship with the sea has defined its history and permeated its culture, with the coast a dynamic, thrilling and occasionally combative landscape, a place where human endeavour comes up against natural forces. Now, with the launch of the England Coast Path, there's an opportunity to explore all corners of the country's incredibly diverse and frequently stunning shoreline on foot. The selection of day and weekend routes in this book have been carefully compiled to capture the essence of the new trail, dipping into the coastal treasure trove to provide drama, challenge, beauty and relaxation. It presents some old favourites, refreshed and improved to rekindle the inspiration, but also introduces less visited stretches of our seaboard, which yield many wonderful surprises.

Wherever you choose to do it, there's something mesmerising about a walk by the sea. Maybe it's the constant rhythmic movement of the waves or the play of light on the water; perhaps it's how all our senses are engaged, from the crashing noise of the waves and screams of the gulls, the salty smell of seaweed and the crunch of shingle beneath our boots or the smooth sand between our toes. Most of us have deep-seated memories of the coast going back to childhood holidays or excursions. It's a special place to walk.

The 30 walks presented here reflect the amazing variety of habitats and scenery around the coast of England, which means there's very likely something for everyone. Deserted sandy beaches, remote shingle spits and wildlife-rich salt-marshes contrast with soaring headlands and rollercoaster cliff

◀ *The England Coast Path has ensured greater public access to the shore (photo: Chiz Dakin)*

paths. There's a little bit of cheeky promenade, some enticing tidal islands and several stunning coastal castles – in other words, the rich, complex and spectacular landscape that is England's very, very long coast.

Geological treasures and coastal landforms

The coast is a great place to appreciate the basics of geology, not least because the rocks are immediate and up close, often exposed in the cliff face right in front of you. Looking down from the coast path at the wave-cut platforms of Robin Hood's Bay, or the folded strata in the cliffs at Hartland Quay, you can see quite clearly what's happened to the rock to make it like it is. Similarly, you can balance on top of the dark dolerite outcrops running across the beach between Seahouses and Bamburgh in Northumberland, or run your hand over the smooth and shiny green stripes of serpentine in the coves of the Lizard. The red sandstone of St Bees Head in Cumbria is as unmistakable as the chalk cliffs of Sussex, where the dazzling white sentinel of Beachy Head and the ripples of the Seven Sisters are as fun to stride across as they are jaw-dropping to stand beneath.

But, as the rocks of the shoreline are revealed, so too are other secrets, such as fossils millions of years old on the beaches of North Yorkshire and the so-called Jurassic Coast of Dorset and east Devon. At Lulworth, the sea has gradually worn away the less resistant rocks to create stunning natural land-forms, including arches, stacks and an almost perfectly rounded bay. Elsewhere, on Cornwall's north coast near Padstow, caves have been carved out by the waves or fashioned into spectacu-lar blowholes, booming every time the water rushes in. If every schoolchild had the chance to witness first hand Round Hole on Trevose Head, or the Devil's Frying Pan on the Lizard peninsula, at full throttle, it's possible that GCSE Geography might be the most popular subject on the curriculum.

The richness of the English coast lies in its wide vari-ety of landforms, and every outing in this book allows you to put in place another captivating piece of the English coastal jigsaw, whether it's the unique vegetated shingle foreland of Dungeness or the pencil-thin sand spit of Spurn Head; Norfolk's vast patchwork of saltmarshes or the muddy creeks of Essex that wriggle like the eels that make their home there. Then there's Morecambe Bay, the UK's largest expanse of intertidal mudflats and sand; or the remarkable (and growing) sand dune system on Merseyside's Sefton coast. In complete contrast is

Exmoor's remote and wild coastline, with not only the highest sea cliffs in England, but also the most extensive broadleaved coastal woodland anywhere in the country. There is simply no better way to understand the make-up of our stunning shoreline, its contrasts and complexities, than to lace up your boots and walk it.

An ever-changing coastline

Somewhat paradoxically, the one constant with the English coast is that it is always changing. Perhaps the most startling manifestation of this is the walk at Dunwich, on the Suffolk coast (Walk 24), where one of the country's leading medieval ports was simply washed off the map by the destructive power of the sea. There are more recent and equally tragic reminders of what the elements can do, such as the storm surge of 1953 that caused devastating flooding along England's east coast and took the lives of over 300 people. The walk around Start Point in Devon (Walk 14) also visits the site of the former village of Hallsands, which disappeared into the sea one night in January 1917.

Of course, given our maritime climate and position on the edge of western Europe, storms and gales are not uncommon, and certainly not for coastal communities in the path of the Westerlies that regularly rattle in off the Atlantic. It's usually a good idea to pack a raincoat or windproof on most coastal outings.

On some of the walks you can appreciate how the sea actively shapes the setting and profile of the shore, such as the constantly changing channels, mudflats and shifting sandbanks of Morecambe Bay. On the North Sea coast, recent storms at Spurn Head by the mouth of the Humber have seen the sea wash over the narrow spit, potentially creating a new tidal island in the same way that you can walk across to Hilbre Island from West Kirby on the Wirral at low tide.

This sense of constant flux is no doubt accentuated by the fact that Britain has the second highest tidal range in the world, at its most extreme in the Bristol Channel where the difference between mean low and high tide is almost 15m (and even over 9m as far along as the Exmoor coast).

Over the years much effort has been put into repelling the sea, building ever more robust barriers to defend the land from watery incursion. But, as climate change has accelerated, modelling by the Met Office has predicted that in a worst

case scenario sea levels might rise by up to one metre in some coastal locations by 2100, potentially submerging vulnerable parts of England's east, south east and north west coasts. As an alternative to hard engineering, there's growing interest in approaches which work with the sea, not against it. Nature-based solutions include so-called managed retreat, where a coastal defence is deliberately breached to allow the sea to periodically flood pockets of low value grazing land. This forms a natural buffer and dissipates the energy of the waves, as well as being relatively low cost and also of significant benefit to wildlife.

This more enlightened and realistic response to the inevitability of coastal change, whether from rising sea levels or the impact of more frequent and fiercer storms, can also be seen in how the England Coast Path itself is being aligned and subsequently managed. The legislation includes a 'roll back' provision ensuring that the trail can adapt relatively easily in the event of coastal erosion or realignment – more details on this in the later section Evolution of the England Coastal Path.

Nature and wildlife

One of the joys of walking along the English coast is its rich natural history, and because coastal habitats are so varied the plant life, in particular, is especially diverse. The tidal marshes of Norfolk and Essex are home to salt-tolerant plants such as shrubby seablite, sea lavender and glasswort; while sea kale, sea pea and yellow horned poppy are a feature of the vegetated shingle of Dungeness and Orford. Near Southport, Ainsdale's

▲ *The vulnerable shoreline at Kilnsea, near Spurn Head (Walk 26)*

sand dunes and the damp hollows behind them support a surprising wealth of insects and flowers, including orchids, bog pimpernel and the rare field gentian, but they're perhaps best known as a stronghold for the sometimes noisy natterjack toad. As you walk out across Dunwich Heath in Suffolk or Lizard Downs in Cornwall, watch out for adders basking in the sun; while gazing seawards from the Cornish clifftops you may be rewarded with the sight of cetaceans like dolphin, porpoise and several different types of whale. The western approaches to the English Channel are especially rich in marine life, including seals, but for an up-close encounter to see one of England's largest grey seal colonies join a licenced boat trip to Blakeney Point in Norfolk.

Many of the walking routes in this book, including along Norfolk's fantastic shoreline, pass a string of top-level nature reserves that are well known for birdlife, in particular. The Flamborough Head walk in North Yorkshire (Walk 27) ends at the RSPB's Bempton Cliffs reserve where, each summer, an estimated quarter of a million birds create the most wonderful sight, sound and (to an extent) smell of any native wildlife spectacle. Other coastal sites are no less important for birds, including breeding gulls and eider ducks on Walney Island in Cumbria; nesting Arctic and Little terns on the beaches of County Durham and Northumberland; and a variety of wildfowl and waders in the Dee Estuary off the Wirral, including bar-tailed godwit, shelduck, egret and redshank.

Given that the coast is such an important natural habitat, it's no surprise that it's awash with protective designations, too. Six national parks have coastlines: Exmoor, South Downs, New Forest, North York Moors and a tiny part of the Broads and Lake District; and what's known as Marine Conservation Zones offer some limited safeguards for the offshore environments and species.

Some of the walks in this book chart ornithological success stories. Avocets were once extinct from our shores but their successful return is associated with Havergate Island, off Orford in Suffolk, where they still nest. Likewise, Cornwall's emblematic county bird, the chough, can be seen once more along the cliffs between Pendeen and Penzance after a long period of absence.

However, in common with biodiversity loss generally, many species found on our shores and in our seas are in serious decline. Pressure on nature around the coast is relentless, whether from development, recreation or pollution, and with climate change and population growth it's a problem that is only likely to increase. Indeed, it's been a delicate balancing act for Natural England, the Government's agency tasked with developing the new trail, as it juggles its twin statutory responsibilities for nature protection and public access, trying to plot the route of a coastal path that will allow people to enjoy open air recreation via some of the most sensitive conservation sites in England.

An island history

Ever since Britain became an island, the sea has played an integral part in our unfolding history. As the sea provides a protective barrier, so the coast defines our physical boundary. Invasion and defence are etched into our collective national psyche, whether it's succumbing to marauding Vikings and conquering Normans or resisting the Spanish Armada and providing the backdrop for Battle of Britain heroics.

Coastal headlands have always provided key defensive sites, from Iron Age promontory forts like Kendijack on the cliffs of west Cornwall, through to the string of sturdy castles on the Northumberland coast that have withstood sieges, feuds and wars. Dover Castle, at the end of Walk 21, can trace 1000 years of history, including its role as a command centre during World War 2. Indeed, standing on the White Cliffs of Kent on a clear day continental Europe seems within touching distance. From the same era come the pillboxes and lookout points on the slopes above Croyde and Woolacombe in Devon, where Allied soldiers practised for D-Day; and observation posts on St Anthony Head, near Falmouth, where beady eyes scanned the waves for enemy craft.

Going a little further back in history, Martello Towers (such as at Seaford and Eastbourne in Sussex) are a peculiar defensive feature of England's south east and Suffolk coast when the threat of invasion was from Napoleonic forces. Equally odd is Bull Sand Fort, marooned in the middle of the Humber Estuary off Spurn Head, built during World War 1 to repel wartime invaders who never came.

Coastal lookouts have had many different motives over time. Fishing folk once stood on the Cornish cliffs to spot massive shoals of pilchards, until over-fishing wiped them out. Lighthouses still warn ships of the dangers of our often notorious inshore waters, and although the 60 or so that remain

Seabirds on Bempton Cliffs, north of Flamborough Head (Walk 27)

around the UK's shores today are all automated, volunteers from the National Coastwatch Institution keep watch from key clifftop locations, such as Prawle Point and St Aldhelm's Head on the south coast. Of course, not everyone has been as altruistic. The coast was for a long time a place where smugglers sought to evade the watchful eye of the excise men, and also where beach scavenging was a commonplace activity for coastal communities – with a modern twist that you'll learn about on the walk at Branscombe in south Devon (Walk 15).

Inevitably, as an island nation, a tradition of seafaring runs deep. It's given rise to great explorers like Captain James Cook, whose life is charted on the North Yorkshire walk (Walk 28), as well as a powerful Royal Navy. The fleet is now smaller but its capability no less deadly, as witnessed from the route around Walney Island (Walk 2) where you can look across to the huge naval shipyards of Barrow where nuclear submarines are built.

Some human activity on the coast is more mysterious. Hidden away at Orford, on the remote Suffolk coast, secretive radar surveillance and weapons trials once took place, including testing nuclear resilience. The site is now deserted and nature is reclaiming the atmospheric shingle spit. Meanwhile, in 1998 on a remote Norfolk beach, a 4000-year-old Bronze Age timber circle dubbed Seahenge was uncovered by shifting sands; but what it was for will never be known. Time and tide evidently wait for no man.

▶ *New Brighton lighthouse (photo: Wirral Council, Walk 6)*

Trade and industry

The days that Britain 'ruled the waves', if indeed it ever really did, might be long gone, but many of our well-known ports expanded in the unprecedented period of growth from the mid 18th century into the modern cities we see today. At the start of the walk around the Wirral you can look across at the famous port of Liverpool, with its state-of-the-art deep-water dockyards and rows of massive cranes. Further up the coast, Lancaster enjoyed a brief heyday two centuries ago and you can trace its maritime history in its architecture and through an excellent heritage centre. But although the days of Empire brought wealth and prosperity, it also left a more troubling legacy of the Slave Trade, which coastal communities here (as elsewhere) are coming to terms with.

As you explore the coast it's clear that plenty of people still make a living from the sea. A large fishing fleet is still based at Newlyn, near the end of the west Cornwall walk outside Penzance; the walk across St Bees Head in Cumbria starts at Whitehaven, a Georgian town with a busy marina; you can gaze down from the White Cliffs in Kent on cross-Channel ferries zipping in and out of Dover's Eastern Docks like clockwork; and the pleasure craft business seems to be booming in Chichester Harbour, which boasts a resident fleet of over 12,000 boats.

The coast has also been the focus for heavy industry and several walks in this book explore sites associated with coastal quarrying and mining. The quarries hewn out of the Dorset cliffs near Swanage several centuries ago have produced highly prized limestone used to build our most celebrated national

▲ *Fishing boats at North Sunderland harbour at Seahouses*

edifices, including cathedrals and royal buildings. The north Cornwall coast was once a world leader in the production of tin and copper and walking through the relics of this former industrial landscape is as instructive as it is haunting.

Much more recently, in fact barely 20 years ago, the coast of County Durham north of Hartlepool was disfigured and black, a result of coal spoil being dumped there from nearby collieries. Then, as with Dorset limestone and Cornish tin, industrial activity ceased, leaving behind seemingly deep environmental scars. But, in a heart-warming story that makes this coastal walk so uplifting, an ambitious programme of regeneration has breathed new life into the coast and has turned it from black back to green. Today you're more likely to find the former shipyards of the north east assembling components for giant wind

farms, which are now such a common sight in our offshore panoramas. Just as the direct impact of climate change is being felt on the physical shoreline and its communities, so too we can see the move from fossil fuels to renewable energy being played out from the coast path.

A coastal culture

There's no doubting that the sea has had a deep and lasting influence on British culture, and the ways in which we have used (and sometimes abused) the coast reflects the paradoxes and extremes of how we live our lives. From St Aidan's 7th-century monastery at Lindisfarne on the coast of Northumberland and the spread of Christianity in Britain, all the way through to the millions of fun-seeking holidaymakers who flocked to

▲ *The English coast has become synonymous with holidays, escape and fun, such as here at Weymouth*

Blackpool's Golden Mile twelve hundred years later; from the National Trust's hugely successful Neptune Coastline campaign that has safeguarded over 570 miles of unspoilt coastline, through to the sewage discharges, military ranges and nuclear plants that disfigure the shoreline and disbar public access.

Certainly the English still seem to regard themselves as a sea-going nation, even though the national fishing fleets and navy are much diminished; but just as the oceans provide livelihoods and opportunities, they also bring danger. The UK and Ireland's 238 lifeboat stations have a proud history, and yet coastal folklore is studded with tales of tragedy and destruction. One estimate puts the number of ships that have sunk off Cornwall alone at over 600.

Despite this, over the last couple of hundred years the coast has become synonymous with holiday, fun and escape. Sandcastles, crabbing and promenading at one end of the spectrum and surfing, coasteering and kite boarding at the other; not to mention the enduring passion for messing about in small boats. There may be less enthusiasm for the restorative powers of saltwater these days, and foreign beaches with more dependable warmth and sun have become more enticing, but according to Visit England's research around a third of all domestic holiday trips are to the coast (pre-pandemic figures). The coast is most definitely lodged in our cultural make-up. Fish and chips have become one of our national dishes, even though as you'll find on the walks in this book there are equally delicious local offerings, from dressed crabs at Cadgwith on the

Lizard, to samphire on the Norfolk coast and kippers at Craster in Northumberland.

Literary associations with the coast abound, whether it's Daphne du Maurier in Cornwall or Bram Stoker's *Dracula* in Whitby. The creative inspiration of being beside the sea is manifested on the Hartland walk in north Devon by a solitary poet who shut himself away in a clifftop shed to compose; and even by a coastal vicar who took to dressing up as a mermaid.

Perhaps the most visibly arresting sight on a number of coastal walks are public art installations. They're playful but often poignant, including the *Horden Butterfly* on the County Durham cliffs that celebrates both nature reborn and the death of a traditional local industry; camouflaged metal songbirds on a Walney Island gate that represent human and natural fragility; and Antony Gormley's 100 iron men staring out impassively from the Merseyside waves at Crosby.

The tremendous variety of the English coastline is also played out in its resident communities, where wealthy modern marinas and retirement villages contrast with ex-industrial communities and trailer parks of genuine poverty. From remote fishing villages to bustling modern ports, noisy seaside resorts to sprawling caravan sites, the England Coast Path (in its entirety) embraces our whole coastal culture; and it's all the more wonderful for that.

Evolution of the England Coast Path

Origins of the trail

People have always walked the shores, whether for work or to trade, for beachcombing or simply to connect communities. Some coastal paths, such as the clifftop routes in Devon and Cornwall, developed as law officers kept a lookout for smugglers. Walking purely for leisure is a relatively modern phenomenon, but although there are newly created sections of the England Coast Path National Trail, it's by no means a brand new route. In many instances the trick has been simply to join up existing trails and improve what's already there. Some of these long-standing coastal paths are already very popular and for years have offered superb coastal walking, including National Trails like the South West Coast Path (fully opened as far back as 1978) and the Norfolk Coast Path, a significant part of the Cleveland Way and a small section of the South Downs Way. In addition, there are a number of regional coastal walking trails

A WIND
THAT CARRIES
MEMORIES
OF COAL

▲ *One wing of the Horden Butterfly art installation (Walk 29)*

COAST PATH
DURDLE DOOR 1
RINGSTEAD 5
WEYMOUTH 10½
MINEHEAD 602

Peter Scott Walk around some of The Wash near King's Lynn, the Bournemouth Coast Path and the Durham Coast Path.

All of these different paths and trails reflect a deep sense of attachment to the coast and the enduring popularity of recreational walking by the sea. So when, in 2000, the Countryside and Rights of Way Act brought in new access rights to the mountains, moorland, heathland, downland and common land of England and Wales, it was perhaps inevitable that attention would then turn to the one omission (apart from woodland) from the list – the coast. Several years of campaigning by the Ramblers, among others, eventually led to further legislation that paved the way for greater public access to the English coast and a new walking trail.

The momentum for change was probably helped by the formal launch of the Wales Coast Path in 2012. Although it was created entirely separately, by the Welsh Government, the realisation of a continuous trail stretching 1400km (870 miles) from Chester to Chepstow showed what was possible and had made Wales the first country in the world to create a dedicated footpath along its entire coastline. However, the legislation that enabled a Wales Coast Path to be developed didn't create any new access rights and so the route had to rely on existing paths close to, but not always on, the actual coastline. Regardless, it was widely noted that in just the first year after the Wales Coast Path opened, coastal walkers spent an estimated £84m in the local economy that supported more than 1000 jobs.

So, with plenty of existing coastal trails in place, the framework for a continuous coastal path around England was already there. Admittedly, there were quite a few gaps, inconsistencies and a few knotty problems to sort out, not least existing land use. Most of England's coast isn't wild and undeveloped but instead is owned and used for specific purposes, often commercial or residential, so that the needs of these owners and occupiers had to be weighed against the rights of people to access the land. Then there was the small matter of internationally important nature reserves, live military firing ranges, oil and gas terminals, major ports and the odd nuclear power station, plus some very large estuaries. All Natural England's coast path team had to do was try and thread it together.

How the route was developed

The power to create a continuous coast path around the entire shoreline of England was set out in the Marine and Coastal

now unified or formalised by the new England Coast Path. Some were developed by walking groups, even individuals, others by partnerships and local authorities, and although they were sometimes along rather than always on the actual coastline, they all provided a great coastal walking experience.

Some of the other regional coastal trails now embraced either wholly or in part by the England Coast Path include the Cumbria Coastal Way, the Lancashire Way, the Solent Way, the Suffolk Coast Path and the Northumberland Coast Path, plus some of the Saxon Shore Way that traces the early coastline of Kent. And, since the England Coast Path extends to the Isle of Wight, there's also the splendid round-island coast path.

Even more locally, there are a few shorter coastal walking routes that now form part of the overall trail, such as the

▲ *The popular South West Coast Path at Lulworth (Walk 16)*

Access Act 2009, with detailed guidance provided in the subsequent Coastal Access Scheme, approved in 2013. It defines a coastal margin in which the new trail sits and where there's provision for what's called spreading room. The regulations also allow for the line of the path to be rolled back in the event of unexpected erosion like a cliff fall, since the existing legal mechanisms for moving a public right of way even just a short distance are complex, time-consuming and often costly. This roll back could even be into an area not originally included in the coastal margin. At a stroke this allows Natural England the flexibility to re-route the new National Trail in response to environmental change or realignment of the shoreline; but it also gives users a better quality experience by enhanced access rights and in all likelihood the best possible walking route. This accessible coastal margin usually covers land (with exceptions) seawards of the path, such as foreshore, beach, dune, cliffs and banks, and is shown by pink shading on Ordnance Survey mapping.

It's clear that the England Coast Path – and hence the walks in this book – are more than simply a line on a map or a solitary route across the ground. There's a defined freedom to explore beaches, rocky foreshore and clifftops, and to sample the many unique habitats that make up the English coast. But remember – just because the map says you can go there doesn't mean it's always safe to do so! Some of the routes in this book (such as Walk 3) visit potentially dangerous coastal areas, and safety warnings should always be taken seriously.

Naturally enough, certain types of land are exempt from this new coastal access, even in the spreading room, so that the new coast path deviates around the curtilage and gardens of private buildings, industrial facilities, schools, aerodromes and military firing ranges. Across most arable farmland, golf courses and caravan and camp sites the trail has to follow a narrow access strip (where practical); and short and long term exclusions may be necessary for conservation reasons where wildlife or habitats are particularly vulnerable. Local access restrictions can also include areas of saltmarsh and mudflat that are not suitable or safe for public access. For more details on public access and up to date information on exclusions and diversions go to the England Coast Path National Trail website (see Appendix A).

The Coastal Access Scheme may have been well thought-out, but inevitably the task of creating a continuous route

around the entire coast of England was an enormous undertaking. It began hopefully, with the first stretch, between Weymouth Bay and Portland Harbour, opened in June 2012 in time for the London Olympic sailing events. Around the coast, volunteers from the Ramblers began carrying out vital work meticulously surveying the routes on the ground. But it still took two years for

▲ *Wildflowers by the path near Lizard Point (Walk 12)*

on legal process delayed progress; and then the small matter of a global pandemic came along, which set everything back even further. Despite this, work to develop the route continued and, section by small section, the new National Trail began to join together and take shape (although as a complete, continuous walking route it's not yet fully open).

The total and precise length of the England Coast Path National Trail is 4499km (2795 miles), making it the longest coastal path in the world. Just as the Land's End to John o' Groats journey provides an irresistible lure to adventurous and ambitious walkers, it's quite likely that this mammoth coastal trail will become the ultimate English long-distance walking challenge, whether in a continuous outing or in more manageable instalments. But in fact a surprising number of people have already embarked on this journey and in some cases have written accounts of their epic coastal journeys (see Appendix B). There may not have been a continuous waymarked trail for them to follow, but (to paraphrase the title of one very good book), all you really need to do is keep the sea on your left. Or your right, of course.

How to use this guide

Clearly any trail of around 4500km offers many, many opportunities for short walks, whether for a few hours or over several days, and especially around a coast so accessible and familiar as England's. So treat the 30 walks in this book as a VIP introduction to the England Coast Path, a hand-picked selection of day walks and a few enticing weekend routes that mix some of the well-known premier league coastal locations with others that will be less familiar – and, in particular, are now accessible and improved thanks to the new coastal path. They will give you both a flavour of this exciting and ambitious National Trail, and showcase some of the truly fabulous walking that is on offer around England's lengthy shoreline.

The 30 routes include some that are unashamedly adventurous and thrilling, where your legs really will be stretched and your head for heights tested; there are other walks, including clifftop paths and gentle waterside routes, that are shorter and more accessible for different ages and abilities, but no less rewarding for all that. The route summary table will help you make your selection. Start by cherry picking the walks that excite your interest, whether it's birdwatching, geology, folklore, lighthouses, local food, ships, flowers, mining, military or art

the next section to be open (34km from Allonby to Whitehaven in Cumbria) and the prospect of meeting the 2020 target for overall completion looked more and more unlikely. The government body tasked with the job, Natural England, was stretched and under-funded before it even began, although after 2014 more resources came their way. A European Court judgement

and literature; then go on to explore places you don't know so well, but which the England Coast Path has helped open up. Wherever you choose to walk you won't be disappointed.

Getting around

Most of the walks in this book are accessible by public transport, and where they are not it is likely to require careful planning. However, a significant number of routes are deliberately designed to be walked using a return bus or train. Check timetables in advance, as these are subject to change and outside the main holiday season (generally Easter to October) some operators are likely to run a reduced service, but timetables are easily available over the internet or via websites like www. traveline.info. Quite apart from lowering your carbon footprint and reducing local traffic and parking congestion, riding a bus or train after a long day's walk can be a supremely relaxing and enjoyable experience. There are also some excellent coastal services that deserve your patronage, including railways like the Cumbrian Coast Line and Merseyrail's Northern Line from Liverpool to Southport, and dedicated bus routes such as the Coaster bus service in Sussex, Coasthopper along Norfolk's shores and the open-top Atlantic Coaster around Cornwall's Land's End peninsula.

When to go

That the coast is open and walkable all year round is obvious enough, but there are seasonal factors that should be taken into account when following the coastal trails. High winds and storms can make all types of seaside walks problematic, especially on clifftops, but inevitably these are accentuated in winter when daylight hours are shorter and temperatures lower. Outside of the summer months the paths in popular areas might be less busy, but before Easter and after October cafés and visitor centres can be shut, and public transport options more limited. This also applies to smaller ferry crossings, which are used by several walks in this book. All that said, a bright spring day or crisp conditions in winter can make for a delightful coastal walk – just make sure you plan ahead and are well equipped.

It's also worth noting that in some places the England Coast Path will have seasonal sections, where for example the most seaward route is closed during the bird nesting season. Check with the National Trails website (see Appendix A) before you set off.

What to take

Like the coastlines they traverse, the walks in this book vary enormously, from gentle beach and waterside rambles with hardly any elevation to demanding cliff paths incorporating steps and steep slopes. Dress according to the terrain, length of walk and anticipated weather. For short, low-level routes in summer, walking shoes or even sports sandals might be appropriate, but walking boots offer more grip and protection on uneven slopes and gradients and are usually more comfortable over longer distances.

Always pack an extra layer and waterproof coat, as the weather on the coast can be unpredictable, even in the summer, and mild sea breezes can turn stronger very quickly.

Walking beside the sea can be delightful on hot and sunny days, but make sure to take a cap or sun hat, sunscreen, and even sunglasses, as coast paths are often open and exposed and the water can give off a reflective glare. A small towel can be a useful addition to your rucksack, if not for a dip (remember to pack your swimming costume!) then at the very least for the pleasure of cooling hot feet with a paddle.

Carrying refreshments, especially sufficient drinks, always makes a walk more pleasurable, but for a few of the routes that are away from any facilities it is essential.

Finally, every rucksack should contain a basic first aid kit. Some of the walks in this book are across relatively remote and difficult terrain, so it makes sense to be properly prepared – if not to help you, then to assist someone else.

Access and waymarking

The starting point for up to date information about the England Coast Path National Trail is the official website www.national-trail.co.uk/en_GB/trails/england-coast-path/trail-information.

Here you will find the latest news, including details of any route diversions and seasonal or tidal alternatives, as well as general advice and background information.

The coast path is designed to be first and foremost a walking route, not for horse riding or cycling. No vehicles (other than mobility vehicles) are allowed and there are no new rights to camp or light fires. Dogs are required to be 'under effective control', in line with new national requirements. This means the owner must keep the dog on a lead or keep it in sight, be aware of its actions and have reason to be confident that the dog will return reliably and promptly on command. There is also a requirement to keep a dog on a short, two-metre lead at all times in the vicinity of livestock. And, since the path goes through wildlife-sensitive sites, there may be local restrictions

walking trails, such as the South West Coast Path, continue to be well signposted.

The route of the England Coast Path National Trail is depicted on Ordnance Survey mapping; and the National Trail website has interactive maps for each section of the path.

GPX tracks

GPX tracks for the routes in this guidebook are available to download free at www.cicerone.co.uk/989/GPX. If you have not bought the book through the Cicerone website, or have bought the book without opening an account, please register your purchase in your Cicerone library to access GPX and update information.

A GPS device is an excellent aid to navigation, but you should also carry a map and compass and know how to use them. GPX files are provided in good faith, but in view of the profusion of formats and devices, neither the author nor the publisher accepts responsibility for their use. We provide files in a single standard GPX format that works on most devices and systems, but you may need to convert files to your preferred format using a GPX converter such as gpsvisualizer.com or one of the many other apps and online converters available.

Staying safe

Although coastal walking is generally safe and fun, it's important to be alert to the state of the tide and not to take risks. Up to date tide tables are widely available, including via the BBC Weather website (www.bbc.co.uk/weather), the Met Office (www.metoffice.gov.uk/weather) or www.tidetimes.org.uk. A small number of featured routes include sections that are likely to be impassable at high tides, so as on any walk don't risk walking on the beach or foreshore if there's a chance that the incoming tide might cut you off, or if weather conditions are rough or changeable.

Some areas of cliff are particularly prone to rock falls, especially after wet weather, so be careful at the foot of cliffs as much as on top, and always obey local notices and follow any path diversions. It's also a good idea be wary of getting too close to the cliff edge when grass slopes are wet and slippery, or when the wind is gusty.

such as on a lead in the bird-breeding season. In some cases, such as the featured walk on Spurn Head, dogs are not allowed at all.

Although there are new waymarks and signposts depicting the route of the England Coast Path on the ground, including the familiar National Trail acorn symbol, given the sheer length of the trail don't expect a continuous string of markers, nor rely on them to find your way. You should still follow conventional rights of way signposts and waymarks (a yellow arrow for public footpaths); and some existing regional and local coastal

▲ *Safety warning on the Seven Sisters cliffs in Sussex (Walk 19)*

North West

Solway Firth to the Dee estuary

The coast of north west England seldom figures among England's top walking destinations, but the crowds that rush headlong for the Lakes or dismiss Lancashire and Merseyside as all resorts and industry are missing out on some real gems. If you like comparatively easy walking along firm sandy beaches and around vast estuaries teeming with birds, this is the place for you. Away from the resorts it's surprisingly quiet with a beauty that gets wilder the further north you travel. Indeed, the unfashionable Cumbrian coastline is bookended by two nature-rich estuaries (the Solway Firth and Morecambe Bay) and in between are highlights such as the red sandstone headland of St Bees (Walk 1) and Walney Island's

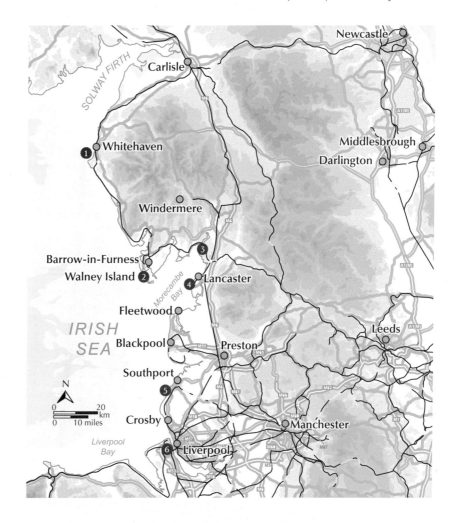

Sunset at Cockerham Sands (photo: Chiz Dakin, Walk 4)

beautiful mosaic of marshes, dunes and windswept sand (Walk 2). St Bees Head aside, the coast is generally low-level and the terrain uncomplicated; and better still the Cumbria Coastal Line makes station to station walks along the England Coast Path very easy.

Heading south, although you could join a Cross-Bay Walk with an experienced guide to cross some of the vast tidal estuary of Morecambe Bay, it's much easier (and drier) to admire it from the coastline. For spectacular views and to really appreciate its enormity, make the easy ascent of Arnside Knott (Walk 3). The sea goes out so far that the mudflats and sandbanks appear to merge with the skyline, but the tide comes back in faster than an adult can run.

After a succession of peninsulas and river mouths the coast straightens out, with the historic port of Lancaster providing a gentle waterside route that traces the lost days of sailing ships and Empire (Walk 4). South of the Ribble is a vast, firm and pristine sandy strip, backed by a huge network of dunes and vegetation alive with insects and flowers, as well as pinewoods where red squirrels make their home. Another efficient local train service shapes a 2-day outing (Walk 5) that finishes with a paddle in the sea at Crosby in the company of Antony Gormley's famous *Another Place* iron men.

From the bustling banks of the River Mersey, the England Coast Path explores the shores of the Wirral on a route (Walk 6) that gets steadily quieter, more scenic and interesting. Hoylake's sandy expanse, a tidal walk to the Hilbre Islands and the backdrop of the Clwydian Range across the peaceful Dee Estuary make this another walk that is likely to change your mind about the coast of the north west.

Steps down to Fleswick Bay, near St Bees Head ▶

Whitehaven to St Bees

Start	Whitehaven (Beacon Museum) NX 969 182
Finish	St Bees (railway station) NX 962 117
Distance	10.5km (6.5 miles)
Total ascent	505m (1660ft)
Time	3hr 30min
Terrain	Cliff path, well defined and mostly level with just a few steeperslopes, as well as open pasture and surfaced tracks
Map	OS Explorer 303/OS Landranger 89
Refreshments	Plenty of choices in Whitehaven, including the café at the Beacon Museum, and Hartley's Beach Café at St Bees
Public transport	Regular daily trains between St Bees and Whitehaven
Parking	Large car parks both ends (charge)

For a walk that mostly revels in the lofty and spectacular cliff scenery of St Bees Head, it's the changing fortunes of a remote west Cumbrian coastal community that first catches the attention. Indeed, relatively few walkers venture beyond the Lakes to the far shores of Cumbria, but the historic port of Whitehaven is beginning to mix its proud Georgian ancestry with modern waterside development rather well. The walking route glimpses its coal-mining past and admires the aesthetic qualities of its distinctive red sandstone, then after soaring with the clifftop seabirds it finishes at St Bees, a popular village probably best known as the start of an epic coast to coast walking adventure. Straightforward and manageable, but always interesting and very scenic, this is an ideal station-to-station to walk using the Cumbrian Coast Line.

From the Beacon Museum, on the southern side of the harbour at Whitehaven, walk along West Strand past the Old Quay in the direction of the open sea. Go past various memorials and sculptures and the remains of Whitehaven Battery to follow the wide surfaced route that winds its way up to the so-called

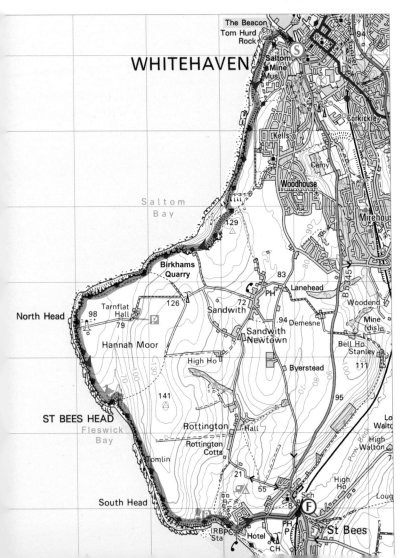

Candlestick on the top of the cliffs. *The Candlestick is in fact the chimney of the former boiler house of Wellington Pit and now provides the town with a notable landmark.*

The popular path continues up the slope beyond the Candlestick and out along the wide clifftop with houses over to the left, including the preserved winding gear and pit-head buildings of the former **Saltom Mine**.

Perhaps **Whitehaven's oddest claim to fame** is that it was once attacked by the USA, although not very much happened and no one got hurt. On the night of 22 April 1778, 30 men from the USS *Ranger* quietly invaded Whitehaven to set fire to British ships moored in the harbour. Under the command of Scottish-born privateer John Paul Jones, they managed to overcome a guard house and start a few small fires, but here the invasion rather fizzled out. According to the English version, some of the American sailors became waylaid by Whitehaven's inviting quayside pubs; or, if you believe the American account, they were hampered by bad weather. Either way, Jones soon retreated to his warship and sailed off. A memorial to this curious episode can be found near the start of the walk.

Keep to the waymarked path that maintains a level course along the clifftop. A lower route has been closed because of cliff erosion. The houses soon disappear and instead there are meadows and fields as the headland draws closer. At a footpath junction stay on the main path straight ahead.

After a short, steep climb the path veers to the left to a path junction. Here take a hard right, almost back on yourself, along a clear route through bracken along the upper slope of the cliff, all the time rising gradually.

The Candlestick above Whitehaven harbour

well as buildings further afield such as Liverpool Cathedral and the V&A Museum in London. As an interesting information board beside the path at the quarry explains, the rich red-brown colour is because the sand grains of which it is made are coated with rust-coloured iron oxide. The highly resistant stone is still much in demand as a building material.

There now follows a lovely section along the level clifftop path, through patches of gorse and heather, with superb sea views. Go through a gate and down across open pasture to enter the RSPB's St Bees Head Nature Reserve. The path rounds North Head then continues below the lighthouse, passing a disused lookout building, and on through open fields along the (fenced) edge of the high cliffs. *The RSPB provide several viewing platforms from where you can watch north west England's only cliff-nesting seabird colony, with fulmars, guillemots, kittiwakes and razorbills all present in the summer months.*

At **Fleswick Bay** the route descends to cross a stream, with excellent views of the red sandstone cliffs immediately ahead. A side path gives access to the stony beach at the foot of the cliffs, otherwise climb back up across open fields to reach **South Head**. Beyond here the flatter coast to the south is revealed, with the village of St Bees almost at your feet; a little

At the very top, 4km after leaving Whitehaven, you reach a bungalow. There are terrific views back to Whitehaven and across the Solway Firth to the mountains of south west Scotland. Follow the signposted path around the outer edge of **Birkhams Quarry**.

The headland of St Bees is known for its distinctive sandstone which was laid down in the Triassic Period, roughly 200 million years ago, when the area was effectively a desert plain. At Birkhams Quarry you can see up close the rich red stone which has been quarried from the area since medieval times and has been used in the construction of Furness Abbey, Muncaster Castle and Barrow Town Hall, as

▲ *Start of the Coast to Coast Walk at St Bees* 31

way beyond are the towers and chimneys of Sellafield nuclear site.

As you gradually descend the slope, divert to the right to reach the remains of a brick coastguard lookout building, where on a really clear day you might be able to pick out Snaefell on the Isle of Man (48km away), Scafell Pike amid the mountains of the Lake District (26km) and south west Scotland (around 40km).

Drop down to cross a footbridge near a caravan park, at the end of the beach, and go left by the lifeboat station. Here you will find a sculpture and information panel marking the beginning of the Coast to Coast Walk.

Alfred Wainwright's well-known **Coast to Coast Walk** links the Irish Sea with the North Sea and begins its journey of around 300km at St Bees. In fact, as Wainwright admits, the walk starts by heading west for the 'lofty bulwark' of St Bees Head, before cutting inland not long after the lighthouse and making its way across to Ennerdale and the western Lake District. Tradition has it that you dip your boot in the Irish Sea before you set off, then finish the walk two weeks or so later by doing the same on the North Yorkshire coast at Robin Hood's Bay. A similar ritual is practised by cyclists setting out from Whitehaven on the equally popular C2C which, depending on your route, runs for 225km across northern England to finish on Tyneside.

The walk emerges at the café by the large car park, with a hotel and pub offering other refreshment choices nearby. To reach **St Bees railway station** (800 metres away) walk out of the car park on Beach Road, then fork right into Station Road.

The Whitehaven story

Perhaps because the Lake District is such a formidable and distracting barrier, the west Cumbria coast often feels rather remote and cut-off. All the more remarkable, therefore, that in Georgian times Whitehaven was the third largest port in England and a hive of industry. Its prosperity was due to the production and export of coal. Collieries ringed the town, so that as you leave Whitehaven on the coast path, you'll pass Wellington Pit (and its Candlestick chimney) and Saltom Mine, which dates from 1729 and was England's first under-sea coal mine stretching 2km from the shore. The streets of the rapidly growing town were laid out on a grid system which, according to some, inspired the grid design of Manhattan in New York City. Some of the fine period buildings of the time remain, albeit a little faded. The Beacon Museum traces the town's evolution from Viking settlement to Georgian industrial and trading centre, then a post-industrial transformation into a nuclear era with Sellafield-financed regeneration. It's quite a journey.

Walney Island

Start/Finish	Walney Island (Biggar Bank) SD 180 671
Distance	26km (16 miles)
Total ascent	180m (590ft)
Time	6hr
Terrain	Flat shingle and sand foreshore, roads and grassy paths
Map	OS OL6 English Lakes SW/OS Landranger 96
Refreshments	Roundhouse Hub & Café at Biggar Bank, the Crown pub at North Scale and Queen's Arms at Biggar
Public transport	Buses from Barrow serve most parts of Walney
Parking	Biggar Bank (free lay-bys)
Note	Seasonal access restrictions apply to small sections of the walk at either end of the island because of breeding birds. Check in advance on the National Trail website and follow the alternative routes as necessary.

There's something very satisfying about walking around an entire island, especially if you can cover it in a day. Walney is England's eighth largest island (linked to the mainland by a bridge) and is long and narrow with outstanding nature reserves at either end. Its beaches, marshes and mudflats are peaceful and extensive, and since most of the island's housing is squeezed into the centre it can easily be bypassed. More than anything, Walney Island is relatively remote, little known and certainly not on Cumbria's mainstream tourist trail, which is why it makes for such a splendid new section of the England Coast Path. In terms of terrain and route finding it's all relatively straightforward; for the inquisitive and connoisseur coastal walker it's an enthralling outing full of interest and discovery.

From the broad grassy strip beside the sea at Biggar Bank on Walney's western shore, with ample off-road parking and the excellent Roundhouse Café, head north to **Sandy Gap**. From here take a public footpath around the edge of the fairways of Furness Golf Club to reach **Earnse Point**. *The huge expanse of firm sand revealed at low tide, as well as a keen offshore wind, makes Earnse Point a popular venue for kitesurfing.*

Continue along the shore track past caravans then turn half right into a low, scrubby area and follow the clear path, keeping the airfield over to your right. At the end cross an asphalt track for a path opposite back to the shore. Turn right and right again to follow a broad track around the far side of a wet and reedy area. Walk alongside the airfield fence and enter **North Walney National Nature Reserve**.

Now home to natterjack toads and an array of birds, the nature reserve also has a poignant human backstory. **Fort Walney** was a former military training camp and later air gunnery school, and although the airfield was subsequently taken over by local shipbuilding firm Vickers (later BAE Systems) the former practise trenches and firing ranges became overgrown as nature slowly reasserted itself. In 2017 a project called 'Fort Walney, Uncovered' brought together artists, archaeologists and the local community to investigate the site and create a memorial to the fragility of both people and nature. Among the art installations is an

◄ *Piel Castle from South Walney (photo: Photo North)*

Black Combe from North Walney (photo: Vivienne Crow)

Lighthouse at South Walney (photo: Vivienne Crow)

a planned estate built in the early 20th century for workers at the shipyard.

Follow residential roads around the outer edge of the estate beside the marsh (Mikasa Street, Avon Street, Orion Terrace, Westminster Avenue), then go left at the end and left again on to Carr Lane. This is the midway point of the walk (around 13km), but such is Walney's elongated shape that you are in fact only five minutes' walk away from where you started on the western shore, should you want or need to shorten your route.

Now walk along Carr Lane for almost 2km to reach the hamlet of **Biggar**. Carry on along the lane and two fields further on go left on hedged path to the shore, then turn right for a short detour around **Copt Hill** (seasonal access restrictions also apply here – check in advance). Otherwise continue along the open lane all the way to **South End** caravan park, enjoying fantastic views of Piel Island and Morecambe Bay.

Go on to the shoreline path to the left of the caravans and at the far side join the open lane. If you want to visit South Walney Nature Reserve turn left and walk along the road to the visitor centre; otherwise turn right and swing northwards once more.

South Walney Nature Reserve is essentially a large shingle island that's home to the only colony of grey seals in Cumbria, as well as important numbers of nesting gulls, terns and eider ducks. The seals are present year-round and at low tide they haul out on the spit at the far tip of the nature reserve (a 'seal cam' has been set up by Cumbria

Wildlife Trust to provide visitors with close-up pictures of these irresistible mammals). The reserve is open daily and there are several waymarked trails and hides that allow you to explore the 130ha site, but dogs are not permitted. Just offshore is the diminutive Piel Island, reached by a summertime foot ferry from Roa Island via the mainland. This privately-owned island boasts, rather improbably, a castle, a pub and a king.

Approaching **Hare Hill**, go left on a waymarked track across the open pasture to the reach the sea (there is no public access to the shore south of here because of breeding birds). Turn right and walk up and across the modest clifftop, with its navigation beacon and wonderful views back over the island to Black Combe and the far Lake District fells. *In the other direction, 19km away in the Irish Sea, is the 659MW 'Walney Extension' which, when it opened in 2018, was the world's largest operational offshore wind farm.*

Now simply walk along the shoreline for 3km, or along the clifftop where waymarked, until you reach the car park at **Bent Haw**. From here, there is a surfaced path along the low clifftop back to **Biggar Bank**.

A walk of contrasts and discovery

Walney Island is an intriguing place full of juxtapositions. Unspoilt shorelines rich in birds, seals and flowers in sight of Europe's largest offshore wind farm and gigantic sheds where nuclear submarines are built. A nondescript housing estate framed against the distant outline of the Lake District fells and the grand sweep of Morecambe Bay. Nature slowly reclaiming the fringes of a former military range and wartime gunnery school. Like Sheppey in Kent and Canvey in Essex (also both on the England Coast Path), Walney may be an unfashionable island destination for a walk, but there are endless surprises. Who knew that Walney is the spiritual home of Thomas the Tank Engine, after the Reverend Awdry modelled the gateway to the fictional island of Sodor on Jubilee Bridge? Or that it has it has its own variety of wild geranium found nowhere else in the world (*Geranium sanguineum var. striatum*)? A true voyage of discovery.

▲ *Deserted beach on Walney Island*   ▶ *Low tide at Arnside (photo: Chiz Dakin)*

Walk 3
Arnside

Start/Finish	Arnside (Promenade) SD 456 788
Distance	9km (5.6 miles)
Total ascent	260m (850ft)
Time	2hr 45min
Terrain	Mostly firm paths and tracks, including a short hilltop ascent, but some potentially soft and wet foreshore and marsh
Map	OS Explorer 307 English Lakes – South-Eastern Area/OS Landranger 97
Refreshments	Cafés and pubs in Arnside, Bob-in-Café at New Barns caravan park (seasonal)
Public transport	Arnside station is served by regular daily trains on the Cumbrian Coast Line; very limited bus service from Kendal (Mon–Sat)
Parking	Arnside Promenade
Warning	Parts of the foreshore as far as Blackstone Point can be impassable at high tide, which rises rapidly, so check timetables online in advance (also displayed on the Promenade)

Morecambe Bay is a vast and unpredictable shape shifter. Perhaps not in terms of solid coastline, but the 310km² (120 square miles) of sand, mud and saltmarsh which forms the UK's largest intertidal area constantly alters as the tide races in and out from the Irish Sea. Five separate estuaries issue out into this shallow lagoon, providing a large-scale interplay of water and light, sea and sky, texture and colour, that gives it an incredible dynamism. Rich in wildlife and natural resources, the sands can be a precarious place for human visitors, as many have found to their cost. Accordingly, this walk skirts safely around the edge, then climbs easily to an elevated viewpoint, revealing the true expanse of the bay.

The walk starts at Arnside pier on the Promenade, where the latest tide tables are displayed. Walk along the pleasant waterfront and head downstream towards the open bay, with the railway viaduct across the estuary behind you. When the path finishes continue past the coastguard rescue station and along the foreshore by **Grubbins Wood**. Approaching **New Barns** swing round to the left to reach the lane and turn right for the entrance of the caravan park, where there is a seasonal café.

The influence of the sea and the irresistibility of the tides seems to permeate so much of this quiet corner of north west England. Until shifting sands and dangerous currents conspired to make the mouth of the River Kent unnavigable, **Arnside** was a working port and a centre for boat-building.

It's said that Arthur Ransome's famous boat *Swallow* was built here in the 1930s and first sailed on the Kent Estuary. The building of the railway viaduct might have impeded ships and helped the estuary to silt up, but it also brought holidaymakers for the first time. Arnside soon developed a reputation as a gentle and picturesque seaside location (a far cry from the brashness of Morecambe on the far side of the bay) – qualities which endure today.

If the tide is too high or rising, follow the inland public footpath signposted Far Arnside which cuts off the first headland – it's straightforward and easy to follow. Otherwise walk back out to the foreshore on the waymarked path to **Blackstone Point**, making your way around the foot of the limestone cliffs and along the part-rocky and sandy foreshore. Grange-over-Sands is in sight, but out of reach, across the estuary mouth.

At low tide and beyond the fringe of salt marsh the bay seems to stretch endlessly into the distance. However, don't be tempted to stray out too far, as Morecambe Bay has a powerful tidal current that sees the water rapidly flood the exposed sand and mudflats. As it rushes up the Kent Estuary it produces what's called the **Arnside Bore**. A bore is simply a large leading wave formed when a strong tide is funnelled into a narrow inlet

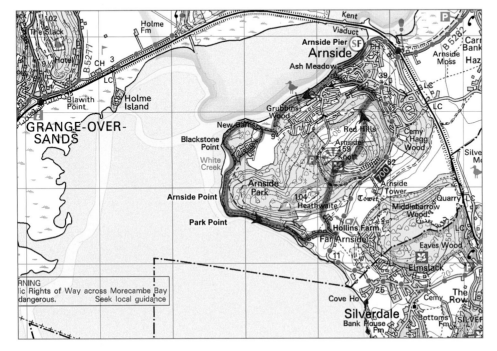

or channel. In the right conditions, such as an exceptionally high spring tide, the bore at Arnside can be almost a metre high. A siren by the coastguard building sounds twice a day (summer only) to signal the start of an incoming tide, a warning previously provided by a bell on the chimney of the Albion Hotel.

Approaching **Arnside Point** scramble up to join the narrow but obvious public footpath that winds its way along the wooded clifftop via **Park Point**. On the far southern horizon is the huge, box-like form of Heysham nuclear power station and before that the resort of Morecambe. *A local delicacy, Morecambe Bay potted shrimps are tiny brown shrimps (not prawns) caught in the bay and cooked in spiced local butter then potted to preserve them.*

Follow the path up to and through a gate to reach a well-screened caravan park. Emerging on to a bend, take the upper driveway and walk along this out of the site and on to a metalled lane. Turn left for a short path signposted Arnside via The Knott,

then left again at **Hollins Farm** to enter the National Trust's Heathwaite estate. Veer right, up the lower slopes of the scrubby hillside, until you reach a gate. At the junction beyond go straight over for the obvious path that winds its way up **Arnside Knott**. Immediately below, to the south east, is the scattered community of Silverdale and Leighton Moss Nature Reserve.

Although **Arnside & Silverdale Area of Outstanding Natural Beauty** covers just 75km² (29 square miles) it includes a wide range of habitats, from limestone hills and pavements through to ancient woodlands, historic orchards and meadows. This in turn supports a wide range of wildlife, including 34 types of butterfly, numerous dragonflies and over half of the UK's flowering plant species, including Lady's-slipper orchid and the Lancaster Whitebeam (which is found nowhere else in the world other than around Morecambe Bay). Apart from the waders in the bay, rare birds such as bittern and marsh harrier breed at the

▲ *The shifting sands of Morecambe Bay (photo: Chiz Dakin)*

RSPB's Leighton Moss reserve. At a time when our biodiversity is under pressure and many species declining, Arnside and Silverdale remains a tiny but much-prized jewel.

Towards the top of the slope, where the path momentarily levels out and dips slightly, fork left for a short diversion through a gate among trees to reach a **viewpoint**, revealing a panorama of the Lake District's southern fells.

Resume the main path across the rounded top of the Knott, with the part-wooded 159m summit over to your right. The main track now dips down the far side to a gate in a wall. Go through this and follow the clear path down the long, open slopes of **Red Hills** pastures beyond, aiming in the direction of

the **viaduct** across the River Kent far below. *The railway viaduct has 50 piers and was built in the 1850s, but then strengthened in 1915 to support the extra weight of the war-time munitions trains to and from Barrow.*

Head down the bumpy hillside and, ignoring a tempting first gate on the right, reach the very bottom corner and go through a gate for a woodland path. At the end of this turn left on to a lane, which you should follow as it zig zags down through houses, turning left at the bottom on to Red Hills Road. Look out for the public footpath on the right, along a private road, that turns into a path back down to the foreshore near the coastguard station. Turn right to return to the start of the walk in **Arnside**.

Crossing Morecambe Bay on foot

Given its size and the strength of local tides, crossing Morecambe Bay on foot is a perilous undertaking and indeed many have drowned over the years. However, since the Middle Ages, when monks from Cartmel and Furness first acted as guides, there have been regular journeys across the soft sands and myriad channels, with travellers and traders led by a local expert, rejoicing in the title of Queen's Guide to the Sands. The first official guide was appointed by the Duchy of Lancaster in the 1500s and one of the most recent, the late Cedric Robinson MBE who retired in 2019, held the post for 56 years. Today organised walking and leisure groups are led across from Arnside to Kents Bank, near Grange-over-Sands. The distance is up to 13km, but because of the shifting sand and variable depth of the channels the precise route is never the same and often requires wading, with crossings even cancelled altogether over safety concerns. You should only cross the bay as part of an organised Cross-Bay Walk led by the Guide to the Sands.

▲ *The Kent estuary and distant Lake District fells from Arnside Knott (photo: Chiz Dakin)*

Lancaster to Cockerham

Start	Lancaster (Maritime Museum, St George's Quay) SD 473 622
Finish	Cockerham (Manor Inn) SD 464 522
Distance	18.75km (11.6 miles)
Total ascent	40m (130ft)
Time	4hr 15min
Terrain	Shared cycle trail, flat field paths and lanes
Map	OS Explorer 296/OS Landranger 102
Refreshments	Numerous cafés and pubs at Lancaster, plus Conder Green (Green Finch café at weekends), Glasson (Lantern o'er Lune Café) and Cockerham (Manor Inn)
Public transport	Regular daily buses between Cockerham and Lancaster
Parking	Roadside on St George's Quay, Lancaster (beyond railway bridge)

A distant windfarm in the sunset off Cockerham Sands (photo: Chiz Dakin)

We tend to associate the golden age of sailing ships with major ports like Bristol and Liverpool; but others, such as Lancaster, also grew prosperous at this time. For around two centuries, large sea-faring vessels regularly made for this corner of north Lancashire from as far afield as the West Indies and the Baltic, bringing a variety of new products and raw materials. But this episode in our past has also left us with the troubling legacy of slavery; and as the easy and level coast path traces the peaceful riverbank and estuary, there are many sobering history lessons for us all.

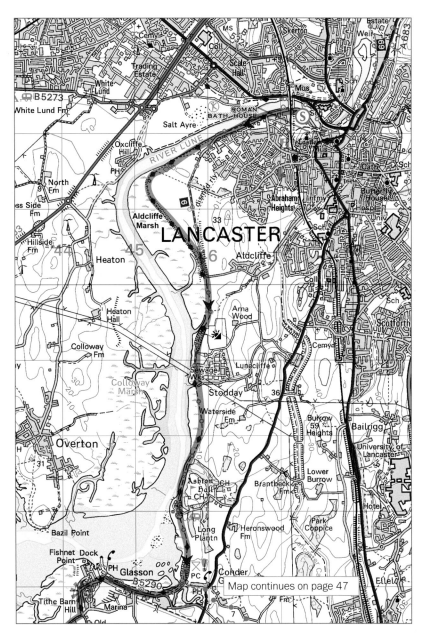

Map continues on page 47

From Lancaster Maritime Museum on St George's Quay follow the pavement beside the **River Lune** downstream until a path branches off through scrub on the right to join the wide grassy riverbank. This is also the route of the Lancashire Coastal Way long distance footpath, which is occasionally signposted.

As the Lune swings south a vast area of saltmarsh opens up. Follow the public footpath at the back of **Aldcliffe Marsh**, either beside or on the top of the embankment. *Across the river is the 350-year-old Golden Ball Hotel, also known as Snatchems because it was supposedly once*

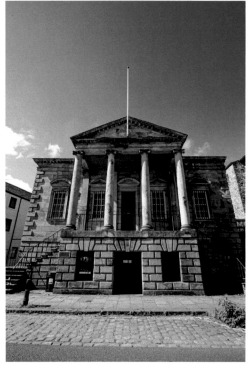

▲ *Lancaster Maritime Museum*

used by press gangs to seize new crew members for outgoing vessels.

Approaching a cross-fence veer left to join a popular shared cycle and walking track along the track-bed of an old railway. Follow this easy and uncomplicated route, the Millennium Park cycleway, for around 5km all the way to **Glasson**. There are sporadic views across the river and nearing Conder Green picnic site you can access the riverside for a short stretch. Beyond the picnic site (where there are toilets) the trail crosses the marsh on a bridge and the unfolding estuary and open sea is finally revealed. Continue into Glasson until you reach the marina.

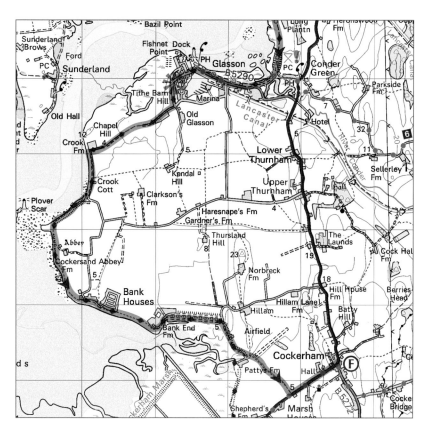

Glasson also owes its development to Lancaster's maritime trade. As the Lune silted up and larger ships were unable to access the city's quayside, Lancaster's merchants instead financed the building of docks at this more accessible location downstream. An arm of the Lancaster Canal was also cut to connect Glasson to the wider network; and later still the railway to Lancaster was built, both to stimulate trade. For some years there was a small shipbuilding yard at Glasson Dock and an information panel on the quayside explains that one of the fifty vessels built here was a schooner called *Ryelands* which among other things was used as the *Hispaniola* in the 1950 film of *Treasure Island*. Although most of the waterborne traffic is now for leisure, Glasson is still a working port and the base for a local grain company.

Cross the lock gate at the outer entrance to Glasson Basin and marina and walk along the road (Tithebarn Hill) past the café. At a junction there is a small knoll with a **viewing area** and helpful direction finder. *Even from this modest elevation there are absorbing and wide-ranging views, including the Lake District's southerly summits, Whernside in the Yorkshire Dales, Lancaster Castle and Winter Hill above Bolton.*

Turn left at the junction, then at the bend go right on to Marsh Lane. Walk past a caravan park and out across fields, aiming just to the left of **Crook Farm**. Here you reach the shore and turn left on to the embankment to follow the farm lane above the estuary.

Across the mouth of the River Lune at Sunderland Point, an isolated location used by early sailing ships, is **Sambo's Grave**. It's the un-consecrated burial site of an African boy who is believed to have been a servant to a ship's captain. He was set ashore in 1736 and died a few days later from an unknown illness, possibly a European disease to which he had no immunity. Some years later a local headmaster, whose own brother was a slave trader, erected a memorial with an inscription that exhorts us to judge 'Not on Man's Color [sic] but his Worth of Heart'. The grave is still visited and tended today. Lancaster Maritime Museum has a display about the city's association with the Slave Trade and how the local community has reflected and responded in recent years.

Continue along an unmade track beyond Lighthouse Cottage, then after a small car park follow a path on top of the sea wall. Go through a gate to enter closely cropped open pasture beside the estuary and 4km after leaving Glasson you reach the remains of **Cockersand Abbey**.

A small, vaulted octagonal building and a few isolated fragments of wall are all that remains of **Cockersand Abbey** – originally a 12th-century monastic infirmary for lepers. Founded by Premonstratensian canons, it was known as the Hospital of St Mary of the Marsh; and as it flourished

▲   *Glasson Dock (photo: Chiz Dakin)*

amid growing support an abbey was added, built out of the distinctive local red sandstone. A simple lighthouse was even constructed to alert vessels to the dangerous mudflats and sand banks. The abbey's fortunes eventually waned and it passed into the hands of the Dalton family of nearby Thurnham Hall. For a while they used it as a family mausoleum, which is why the chapter house has survived and some of the stonework is believed to have been used to shore up the crumbling estuary bank.

Continue along the raised edge of the shore. Ahead is the Fylde peninsula and on the distant skyline you may be able to make out Blackpool Tower. Beyond an old brick lookout building, join a surfaced path that becomes a lane past a caravan site. Stay on the path beside the marshes and go past a second site at **Bank End**. Beyond the large farmhouse walk along the open lane at the foot of the robust flood defence. On your right there are extensive marshes and creeks, with a specially constructed eel pass.

At the junction at the far end go right and continue around the edge of the marsh towards **Pattys Farm**. Just before you reach this, at the parking bay, go left up an embankment and over a stile, then right over another and through a copse. Go ahead across the end of a light aircraft landing strip and follow the left edge of successive fields to reach the road. Turn left to walk the pavement the short distance into **Cockerham**.

The rise and fall of the port of Lancaster

Although it's hard to believe today, Lancaster was once a busy port that for a while rivalled Liverpool for the volume of trade that it handled. Its heyday was at the end of the 18th century, when in a single year 57 ships arrived from the West Indies bringing the likes of tobacco, coffee, sugar and spices; and 17 ships docked from Europe with cargoes of timber, iron, tar and flax. However, rising costs and problems with tides and shallow water for larger ships navigating the River Lune led to its decline. Today most of the riverside warehouses are residential, but there are still a number of fine-looking Georgian properties from the period around the city; and at the grand-looking Custom House on St George's Quay, the city's Maritime Museum (open daily) tells the colourful and at times tragic story of Lancaster's relationship with the sea, from fishing and trade to slaves and smuggling.

Walk 5
Southport to Crosby

Start	Southport (Marshside Nature Reserve) SD 352 204
Finish	Crosby (promenade) SJ 304 991
Distance	31km (19.2 miles)
Total ascent	60m (200ft)
Time	8hr
Terrain	Gently undulating sandy paths, woodland tracks, beach, surfaced promenade
Map	OS Explorer 285/OS Landranger 108
Refreshments	Numerous pubs and cafés at Southport and Crosby, plus Ainsdale and Formby (just off the route), as well as seasonal kiosks at many of the beach car parks
Public transport	With stations at Southport and Crosby (and seven in between), the whole route is served by Merseyrail's fast, regular daily train service
Parking	Plenty of car parks (some charge) or street parking
Note	Although this is an invigorating 1-day walk it can also be made into a more leisurely 2-day affair by breaking the route at Freshfield or Formby (handy railway stations)

The attractive and accessible coastline between the Mersey and Ribble estuaries contains the largest sand dune system in England. Sand dunes play a vital role protecting the coast, but nationally they are under threat, with a third of the UK's dunes declining since 1900. Here, on the Sefton coast, the firm and golden beach gives way to almost 20km of towering dunes, topped by tufts of marram grass. Behind is a semi-vegetated area of scrub, heath and damp hollows that on a sunny summer's day is vibrant with insects, birds and colourful flowers. Throw in a red squirrel colony, a modest but friendly resort and a famous public art installation, and you have an absorbing 2-day walk which, thanks to the excellent local train service, you can adapt according to your speed and itinerary.

The walk starts just north of Southport, at the RSPB's Marshside Nature Reserve by the Ribble Estuary. From the car park at the junction with Marshside Road walk along the edge of the saltmarsh towards Southport and then join the promenade to pass below the pier and on past the Trans Pennine Trail sculpture. *The Trans Pennine Trail is a 346km coast to coast walking, cycling and horse riding route that links Southport with Hornsea, near Hull, and has spurs to Leeds, Chesterfield and York.*

Beyond the new lifeboat station drop down to the shore for a clear path that runs beside the saltmarsh and then threads its way purposefully through the vegetated dunes. Over to the left is **Royal Birkdale golf course** and to the right, beyond the

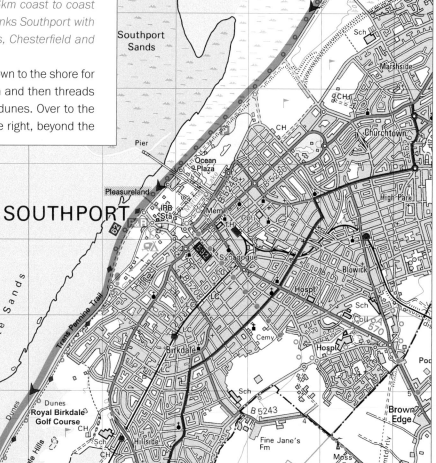

Map continues on page 54

◄ *The dune system on the Sefton coast is the largest in England*

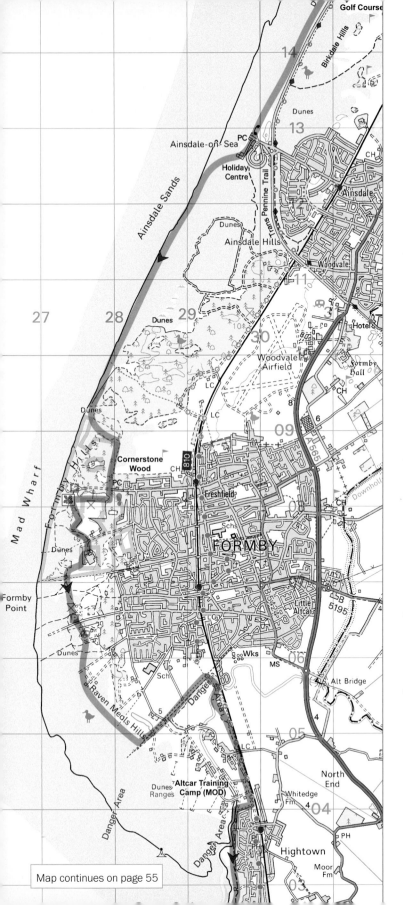

Map continues on page 55

high sand dunes, is the sea. In late spring and summer this lush strip is awash with flowers and wildlife.

Unlike elsewhere on England's coast, parts of the low-lying shore of Sefton are gradually accreting (growing) rather than eroding. Sand dunes are dynamic features, where wind-blown sand is trapped by marram grass and other salt-tolerant plants and over time the vegetated dunes have expanded. This walk visits a succession of important **nature reserves** which, away from the open sand, are carpeted with summertime flowers such as orchids and helleborines. Damp pockets, known as dune slacks, contain yellow flag iris, bog pimpernel and reedmace or bulrush; but, just as importantly, they provide breeding pools for natterjack toads. This part of the coast is a stronghold for Europe's loudest amphibian, with the croaking males (apparently known locally as Birkdale nightingales) being audible over 1.6km away in their attempt to attract a mate each spring.

Arriving at **Ainsdale-on-Sea** after 9.5km, where there are toilets and a seasonal snack bar, either continue on a rather meandering path through the extensive network of sand dunes or, if you want to pick up speed or seek firmer conditions underfoot, switch to the wide sandy beach.

As you progress southwards pine plantations begin to appear behind the beach, a legacy of a century or so ago when landowners tried to stabilise the dunes by mass planting.

Veer inland on a wide track around the back of Freshfield caravan park, or otherwise head east along Victoria Road from the National Trust's beach-side car park, to reach **Cornerstone Wood** (toilets). This is the beginning of the circular Squirrel Walk, named after the pines' resident red squirrels. It's also the route's half way point, at 16km, with Freshfield railway station just 1km further along Victoria Road.

The England Coast Path now heads back out towards the coast by following, at least to begin with, the National Trust's waymarked **Asparagus Trail**. For over a century the area was renowned for producing this delicacy of the vegetable world. The climate, light sandy soils and high water table (requiring little irrigation) produced spears with a sweet

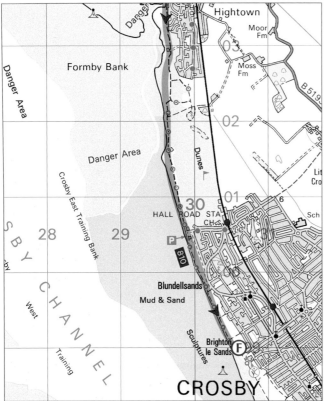

flavour which were highly sought-after. The heyday was in the 1930s, when fresh handpicked bundles were sent daily to Liverpool by train for consumption at home and abroad – it's even rumoured that it was served to passengers in First Class on the *Titanic*'s ill-fated voyage. Recently attempts have been made to revive asparagus-growing at Formby, so if you're walking here in May and June look out for rows of slender green spears.

Follow the main track almost due south through **Ravenmeols Hills** Nature Reserve, past a private hospice and on through Lifeboat Road car park. The open, scrubby land-scape gives way to more pronounced dunes, and from the car park there's a short path up to a viewing platform on top of one of the higher ones. From here you can either continue through the dunes or, better still, make for the open beach and the broad and unbroken sandy strip. At **Formby Point** the shore swings away, revealing the first glimpses of Liverpool's docks.

▲ *One of Anthony Gormley's iron men on Crosby beach*

The giant red and white cranes in the distance have been installed as part of the development of a deep-water container terminal called Liverpool2.

Beyond Cabin Hill Nature Reserve is an MOD rifle range, so the England Coast Path makes a 4km detour inland around the perimeter of **Altcar Training Camp**, including a tarmac cycle path beside the railway, then returns to the shore on a narrow path behind houses. The route joins the banks of the diminutive River Alt, then strides out through the dunes before reaching **Blundellsands** Sailing Club boathouse and slipway. A little beyond this join a surfaced track above the shoreline, where signs for the Sefton Coastal Path are a reminder that an excellent coastal trail has been in place here for many years.

With fantastic views across the mouth of the Mersey to Liverpool, the Wirral (Walk 6) and the hills of North Wales, the walk finishes on the promenade at **Crosby** – or rather, on the beach (tide permitting) in the company of 100 iron men.

Another Place

The well-known art installation created on Crosby beach by sculptor Antony Gormley consists of 100 life-size figures made out of iron, using casts from the artist's own body. They are spaced out over 3km of shoreline, with the furthest almost 1km out to sea, so that as the tide rises and falls the figures disappear or emerge from the waves. Entitled *Another Place*, the installation opened in 2005 amid some controversy, including instances of the coastguard being misguidedly called out to rescue what were thought to be people in distress in the water. Although it was only planned to be a short term project, the iron men have become a popular tourist attraction and a permanent fixture on the Sefton coast, but in 2019 an operation was mounted to recover ten of the 650kg-men, which had been swallowed up by the soft mud as their concrete support piles disintegrated. All are now back in place, gazing out to sea in silent contemplation.

Walk 6

New Brighton to Heswall *(the Wirral)*

Start	New Brighton (Marine Lake) SJ 309 944
Finish	Heswall (bus station) SJ 268 818
Distance	25km (15.5 miles)
Total ascent	100m (330ft)
Time	5hr 30min
Terrain	Flat promenade, sandy beach, firm tracks and saltmarsh
Map	OS Explorer 266/OS Landranger 108
Refreshments	Plenty of choice in New Brighton, Hoylake, West Kirby and Heswall
Public transport	Frequent daily train and bus connections between New Brighton and Heswall
Parking	Car parks at either end
Note	For the tidal walk to Hilbre Island make sure you know the tide times and safe crossing point before setting off, see www.hilbreisland.info

This gentle walk around the coastal fringe of the Wirral, between the Mersey and Dee estuaries, is rather deceptive. Practically speaking it's straightforward and virtually flat the whole way, with plenty of facilities and good transport links. But nondescript it is not. The Wirral might not have the dramatic scenery of other peninsulas, but the England Coast Path takes you on a journey from the colourful and vibrant Mersey of Liverpool to the altogether more serene, scenic and wildlife-rich waters of the Dee on the border with Wales. Depending on the times of the tide, along the way there's the chance to walk across the sands to a tidal island largely unknown to most people beyond the Wirral. The problem is likely to be fitting it all in.

The walk starts at the mouth of the River Mersey at New Brighton, opposite the docks of Bootle, and with the famous Liverpool landmarks just a short distance away upstream. From the car park in front of **Fort Perch Rock** cross the slipway (or inland of Marine Lake if the tide is very high) and head west along the popular promenade. *Fort Perch Rock is a former defensive battery built in the 1820s to protect the Port of Liverpool and apparently nicknamed the Little Gibraltar of the Mersey.*

From here all the way round to West Kirby (15km) you have the option of walking along the surfaced promenade or the wide and firm sandy beach below, depending on the weather conditions and the state of the tide. Further on there's a very pleasant grassy path along the top of the embankment and through the dunes, offering good views.

After 2.3km the road veers away just before an old coastguard lookout tower, and from now on it's a much quieter walk. As the first dunes begin to appear you enter **North Wirral Coastal Park**. Follow this narrow green corridor, sandwiched between the sea and Wallasey golf course, all the way to **Meols**.

Continue via Leasowe Bay and Moreton Beach above the formidable concrete defences of Wallasey Embankment. Offshore, beyond the sandbanks, is a massive wind farm, while landwards is **Leasowe lighthouse**.

Fort Perch Rock at New Brighton (photo: Tony Lamberton) 59

The 6.4km-long **North Wirral Coastal Park** is made up of a string of dunes, commons and meadows that frame the Wirral's straight, sea-facing shore, but even this modest park contains some surprises. Leasowe lighthouse is Britain's oldest brick-built lighthouse, constructed in 1763 by the Mersey Docks and Harbour Board to aid shipping. When it closed in 1908 it had the only known female lighthouse keeper at the time. More recently, nearby Moreton Beach was the site of the world's first passenger hovercraft service, which started running to Rhyl in North Wales in 1963. However, despite initial optimism, bad weather took its toll on the trial and the Vickers-Armstrong VA3 was only operational for 19 out of a scheduled 54 trips, eventually breaking down completely and at one point drifting out into the Irish Sea.

The grassy embankment path ends by the modern coastguard station at Meols and the start of suburban **Hoylake**. Go on past the model boating lake and new lifeboat station, noting the ornate drinking fountain with Queen Victoria reliefs, and on past East Hoyle Bank. *East Hoyle Bank is a vast swathe of firm*

sand and one of the UK's premier sites for land yachting and kite buggying (three-wheeled buggies powered by kites).

At King's Gap the road turns away from the shore and here take to the wide sandy strip below the houses, which is semi-vegetated above the mean high water line, to reach **Hilbre Point** and a close-up view of Hilbre Island.

The route now swings south, along the edge of the Dee Estuary, with Wales just across the water. Either walk the beach or a wide track through the foot of the dunes beside the Royal Liverpool Golf Course (usually just called 'Hoylake') for 2km to reach **West Kirby**, which has the full range of amenities. It is also the departure point for the tidal walk across to Hilbre Island.

From Wirral Sailing Centre walk around the outer edge of **Marine Lake**, an artificial saltwater lagoon popular with

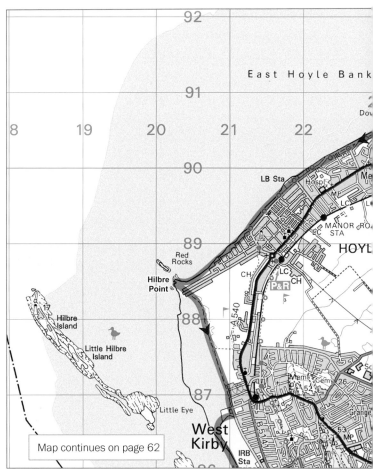

Map continues on page 62

▲ *Low tide off Hoylake (photo: Tony Lamberton)*

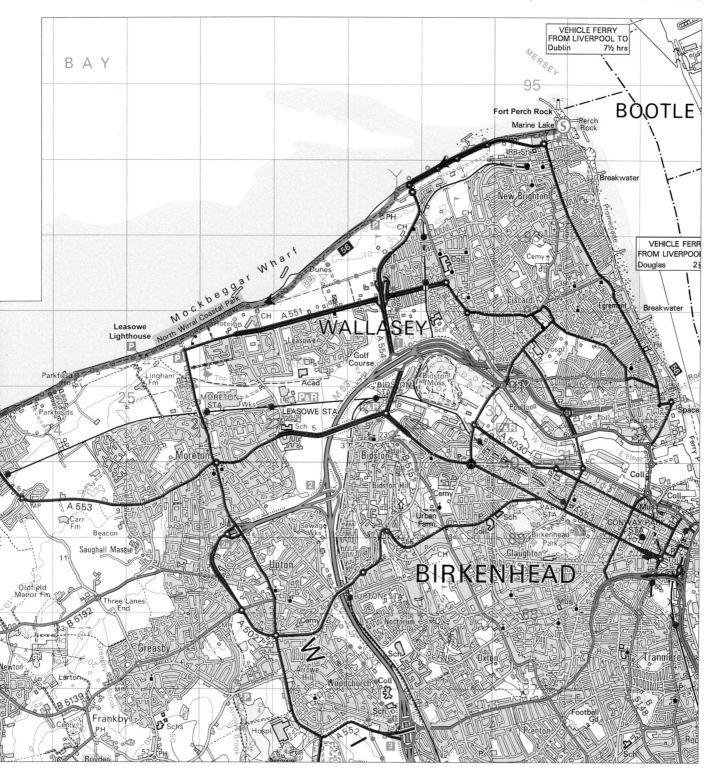

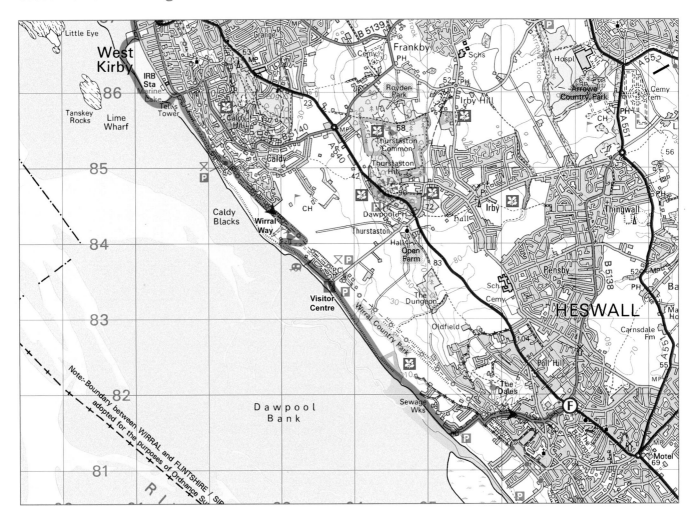

paddleboarders and windsurfers, on a surfaced walkway that may be inaccessible at exceptionally high tides when the sea washes over (in which case take the landwards route).

By the boatyard next to West Kirby Sailing Club follow the pavement inland and turn right along Macdona Drive. At the far end continue across an area of low, grassy clifftop known as Cubbins Green, then via a small car park behind houses to reach a minor road down to the shore. On the far side pick up the **Wirral Way**, a former railway line that is now a shared walking and cycling route, and which runs parallel with the shoreline through Wirral Country Park all the way to Neston.

After 1.5km turn right, off the trail, at the signpost for Dee Sailing Club. Veer right, down the lane past a caravan site, to reach the shoreline just before the clubhouse. Turn left and

walk along Thurstaston Beach at the foot of low cliffs. (If this last stretch to Heswall is impassable because of the tide simply keep to the Wirral Way past the country park visitor centre.)

As you make your way along the edge of the **Dee Estuary** the character of the Wirral changes and the walk takes on a different complexion. Instead of open sea and wind farms the skyline is now dominated by the rolling green shapes of the Clwydian Range across the water. Closer to hand there are low cliffs, made up of a crumby mix of boulder clay, sandstone and gravel, while the sandy expanse of Hoylake and West Kirby is replaced by mudflats and saltmarsh. Compared to the start of the walk beside the busy Mersey,

Hilbre Island (photo: Friends of Hilbre) ▶

this is a peaceful and comparatively unspoilt location, so it's no surprise to learn that the Dee Estuary is one of the most important sites in England for waders and wildfowl. There's more information about what to see and where from the country park visitor centre near Thurstaston.

Continue along the edge of saltmarsh, which may be muddy in places. Just beyond a boatyard, by a restaurant called

Sheldrakes that was formerly the base of the local sailing club, turn away from the Dee and follow the metalled lane inland amid the houses of Heswall until you come to a crossroads. Go straight over on to Dee View Road and at the first bend turn left for a long flight of steps (a public footpath). At the top go right, then left along the pavement, to reach the centre of **Heswall** near the bus station.

A tidal walk to Hilbre Island

The tiny Hilbre Island lies in the mouth of the Dee Estuary 3.2km from the mainland and can be reached on foot at low tide. The main island (there are a few small outliers) has a few buildings, including an old lifeboat station and telegraph station, and today it's managed as a local nature reserve. The views back across to mainland England and Wales are fantastic and the sense of isolation and remoteness is palpable – a real castaway feeling! Hilbre is surrounded by the tide for up to six hours twice a day, so you must time your visit carefully. Tide tables and advice on when to cross are available at West Kirby, where there is a seasonal lifeguard service. The tidal walk takes up to an hour each way and must only be made from West Kirby via the two outlying islets of Little and Middle Eye, not directly from the point at Hoylake, because of deep water channels and mud.

South West

Severn Estuary to The Solent

Due to its mild climate, good facilities and of course breath-taking scenery, south west England has long been a favourite with coastal walkers. Well before the England Coast Path was dreamt up, a continuous walking trail of 1014km (630 miles) knitted this coastline together, stretching from Minehead in Somerset to Poole in Dorset and encompassing all of the coastline of Devon and Cornwall. The South West Coast Path, now part of the overall England route, remains one of the highest quality domestic coastal walking experiences, but despite its popularity the actual walking can be quite varied and it's comparatively easy to escape the crowds.

If you want to test your leg muscles and stamina on lofty headlands or plunging cliff paths, then there are certainly routes here for you. There's no better place to start than with England's highest sea cliffs on Exmoor's wild and remote north Devon seaboard (Walk 7). Further west, the rollercoaster cliff path from Hartland Quay to Bude (Walk 9) is among the most exhilarating but exacting you will find anywhere on England's coast; while switching to south Devon, Walk 14 takes you

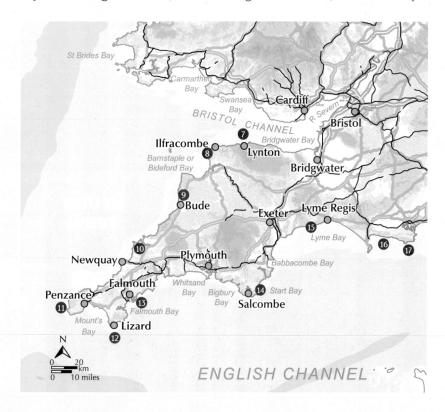

Whitesand Bay from Sennen Cove (photo: Chiz Dakin, Walk 11)

out to Prawle Point and Start Point, two commanding headlands jutting out into the English Channel.

The 2-day clifftop route around the Land's End peninsula (Walk 11) is as accessible as it is enjoyable, capturing so much that is quintessentially Cornish (from tin mines and surfers to pasties and choughs). Even at peak season the crowds never tend to venture far from the honeypots; but elsewhere you can enjoy some high quality waking in relative seclusion, including easy circular walks around the Lizard (Walk 12) and through the part-wooded Roseland peninsula, near Falmouth (Walk 13).

Sometimes it's nice to relax, such as at the end of the circular route around Baggy Point from Woolacombe (Walk 8)

which finishes with a pleasurable (and preferably barefoot) 5km amble along a stunning beach. There's a delightful but uncomplicated clifftop circuit of Trevose Head from Padstow, interspersed with sandy bays (Walk 10); while on the south coast the dramatic chalk cliffs at Beer (Walk 15) and at Lulworth (Walk 16), complete with rock arches, stacks and an exquisite cove, are captivating for all ages. Meanwhile, Walk 17 explores the atmospheric former cliff quarries west of Swanage, in Dorset, which once provided the building blocks for some of our most prestigious buildings but are now used as futuristic film sets. More great stories, more great coastal walking.

Walk 7
Lynton to Combe Martin

Start	Lynton (Town Hall) SS 718 494
Finish	Combe Martin (Kiln car park) SS 577 472
Distance	21km (13 miles)
Total ascent	1305m (4280ft)
Time	7hr
Terrain	Generally firm and broad cliff and woodland paths, but frequently high, exposed and with several steep sections
Map	OS Explorer OL 9/OS Landranger 180
Refreshments	Plenty of choices in Lynton and Combe Martin, otherwise Lee Bay Tea Cottage (summer only) and Hunter's Inn in the Heddon valley are the only other options
Public transport	None currently available so careful planning will be necessary
Parking	Car parks in Lynton and Combe Martin (charge)

Of the three main upland areas in England's south west peninsula, only Exmoor has a coastline – and what a remote and rugged one it is! Not only does it contain the highest sea cliffs in England, but this isolated and surprisingly inaccessible shore also boasts the longest stretch of coastal woodland in England, where steep-sided combes plunge down to the sea in dramatic fashion. It all makes for a spectacular and exhilarating day's walking; but don't underestimate it, either. In places the path is steep and rough, as well as exposed. If it's windy on the top of Great Hangman you will certainly know about it, possibly as you bend double to get across the upper slopes; but you will also come away with some truly superb coastal walking memories.

From Lynton's large and ornate town hall, incorporating the tourist information centre and toilets, go down the main street (Lee Road) through the centre of this official 'Walkers are Welcome' town and turn left on to North Walk Hill. Follow it across a bridge above the Cliff Railway, with stunning views down to Lynmouth far below. *Opened in 1890, the Lynton and Lynmouth funicular Cliff Railway claims to be the highest and steepest totally water-powered railway in the world.*

Now on the waymarked route of the South West Coast Path, carry on past period hotels tucked away in the lush woodland and out along North Walk, a surfaced path that runs along the high and sloping cliff. Unless you want to nip up Castle Rock for the views, follow the coast path signs into the **Valley of Rocks** and on along a path through the bracken, which at the end climbs to join the road. Follow the quiet lane past **Lee Abbey** and **Lee Bay** into woodland. *Since 1945 the listed Gothic buildings of Lee Abbey have been run as an ecumenical Christian community offering retreats, study breaks and holidays for guests.*

After 2km leave the road temporarily for a circuit of **Crock Point**, then less than 1km further on take a well-signposted path on the right above the appropriately named **Woody Bay**.

The route emerges from the oak woodland and crosses the steeply sloping hillside, covered by gorse, heather and

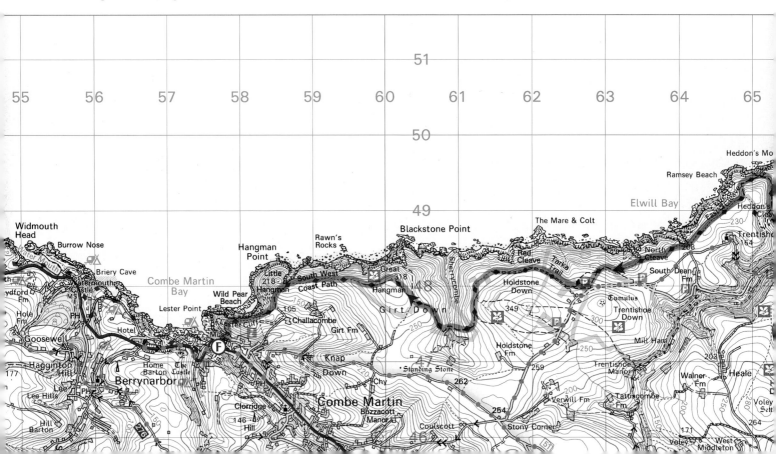

bracken, high above the sea. The path is firm, wide and easy to follow, but it feels surprisingly remote and, weather-permitting, there are far-reaching views across to south Wales.

At **Highveer Point**, with the tiny beach at Heddon's Mouth far below, the rocky sentinel provides a stunning vantage spot.

Follow the path as it swings inland and drops down into the wooded Heddon valley, which is just under half way along the route at 10km. Continue along the valley bottom, heading away from the sea, until you reach a path junction by a stone footbridge. Hunter's Inn is another 800 metres further along this well-used path. *Now owned by the National Trust, Hunter's Inn has been a popular destination for visitors since 1823 and is well-placed for refreshing weary coastal walkers.*

Exmoor's north coast boasts England's longest stretch of continuous broadleaved coastal woodland, between Porlock and Countisbury, dominated by sessile oak and ash, but also including rare whitebeam. It's often twisted and gnarled into amazing shapes and is an evocative and sensuous place through which to walk. Sometimes referred to as Atlantic woodland, this ancient semi-natural woodland

Castle Rock, near Lynton

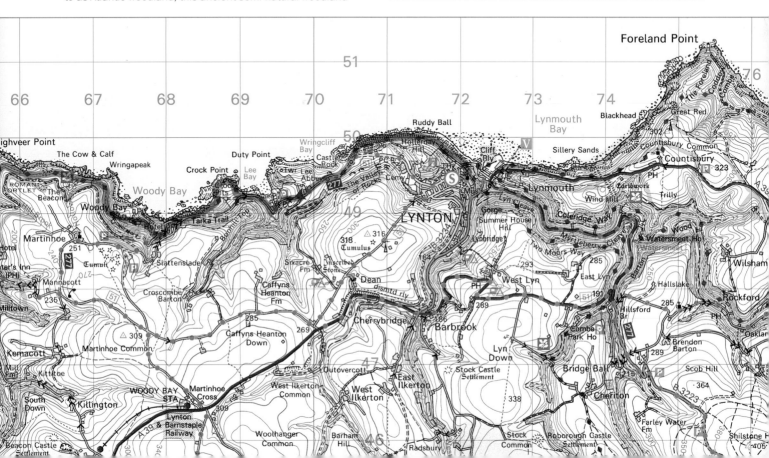

is subject to moist air and a generally mild climate that quite apart from making it rich in insects and attractive for birds such as redstarts and pied flycatchers, also means that it's incredibly important for mosses, lichens, liverworts and ferns. Not only are these valuable in their own right, but they are also useful environmental measures in terms of how clear or dirty our air is; plus they act as early indicators of changes in climate.

Cross the bridge and follow the path as it winds its way up the hillside opposite, sometimes steeply and in places around patches of scree. It finally levels out and returns to the same high-level and exciting route along the upper cliff shelf. The way-marked trail now takes to the open slopes of **Trentishoe Down**, beside a fence. There are more expansive views up and down this plunging coast, as well as inland across the gentle, rolling slopes of Exmoor National Park. The feeling of elevation and

airiness is likely to be palpable, especially if the wind is blowing keenly off the Bristol Channel!

Trentishoe is a particularly peaceful place today, open and ostensibly unspoilt slopes of pasture and moorland, so it comes as something of a surprise to learn that during the 1970s it was the venue for popular outdoor music festivals that lasted for up to three weeks at a time. The festivals, or Whole Earth Fayres as they were called, were about more than just music, however, and instead aimed to encourage an alternative way of life that promoted recycling, renewable energy, organically grown food and shared resources. Many of those attending were family groups and they often built their own shelters, including wigwams and yurts, and organised a range of social activities. The spectacular hilltop location was certainly part of the attraction, but as one festival-goer admitted some of the 'wow, far out' comments might not have been referring to the views.

Arriving at **Holdstone Down** 5km after leaving the Heddon valley, the route swings inland and drops down steeply over bracken-covered slopes to cross a stream. Follow it up the far side as it plods steadily towards the bulky summit of **Great Hangman**, crowned by a low and sprawling mound of stones. *Although the path stays well back from the edge, Great*

▲ *Huge whaleback hills near Trentishoe*

Hangman is a massive coastal barrier and its 244m sheer sea cliffs are the highest in England.

The remaining 3km are gentle and thankfully downhill. Combe Martin is soon glimpsed ahead as the path follows field margins and makes for **Little Hangman**, the top of which is just off the path and can be reached by a short track. Just beyond this there is a very steep permissive footpath down to **Wild Pear Beach**, entirely tucked away at the foot of the cliffs – but you have to come back up the same way.

The route continues to be well signposted as it finally drops down into **Combe Martin** itself, weaving its way between properties before emerging at the Kiln car park and toilets above the beach.

Witches, whites and goats in the Valley of Rocks

The Valley of Rocks outside Lynton is a fascinating but rather odd place. This dry, open valley appears to run parallel to the coast and it's been suggested it represents the original course of the River Lynn before it diverted to its present course through Lynmouth. The valley is ringed by rocky outcrops that wouldn't be out of place in the Peak District or on Dartmoor. They include the White Lady and Devil's Cheese Ring, used by RD Blackmore in his Exmoor-based novel of 1869 *Lorna Doone* as the winter home of white witch Mother Meldrum. At the foot of the valley is the sandstone pinnacle of Castle Rock, while further up is a remarkably sited cricket pitch that is home to Lynton and Lynmouth Cricket Club. More unusually still, free-ranging feral goats wander the valley, as they have done on and off since Domesday times, although public opinion in Lynton is divided between supporters and critics of the goats and their social and environmental impact.

Woolacombe and Croyde

Start/Finish	Woolacombe (Marine Drive car park) SS 457 432
Distance	14.5km (9 miles)
Total ascent	335m (1100ft)
Time	3hr 30min
Terrain	Soft dunes and firm sandy beach, straightforward clifftop paths
Map	OS Explorer 139/OS Landranger 180
Refreshments	Wide choice at Woolacombe, Putsborough and Croyde
Public transport	Daily bus services to Woolacombe and Croyde from Ilfracombe and Barnstaple
Parking	Marine Drive car park, Woolacombe (charge)
Note	There are restrictions on dogs at the Woolacombe end of the beach April to October

Woolacombe and Croyde are two of the most delectable bays on the north Devon coast, gorgeous sweeps of unblemished sand popular with sandcastle-builders and surfers alike. Separating them is the craggy headland of Baggy Point and this relatively easy and family-friendly walk out to its far end is equally delightful. However, the pristine beaches and unspoilt clifftop weren't always like that. In the early 1940s this area was commandeered by the American army which used it as a full scale practice for the Normandy landings and invasion of France. It was a time of great activity but also tragedy; and a reminder that the coast has played many different roles over time.

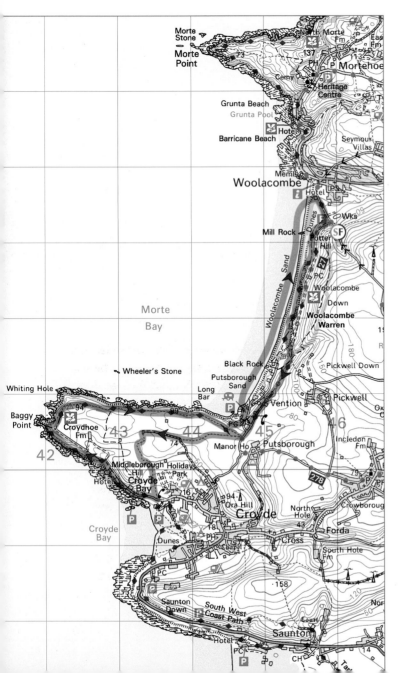

The walk starts at Marine Drive car park on the lower slopes of Woolacombe Down, south of the village, although there are other car parks nearby as well. Drop down through the dunes to the wide and obvious track below, which runs parallel with the sea. Turn left and follow this popular route through **Woolacombe Warren**. Alternatively, you could simply walk to the far end of the car park and keep going, along the surfaced lane above the dunes.

At a junction of routes go left on a signposted bridleway uphill to veer right on to an unsurfaced lane (which connects to the car park). This narrows to a hedged track. Follow the signposted path to Putsborough, high up on the hillside overlooking the bay. Join a tarmac lane and walk past the turning down to Putsborough Sands, then at the brow of the hill go right at the coast path sign.

Just as this beautiful part of Devon was used as a setting to rehearse war, it has also provided an escape from such horrors. In 1921 and utterly disillusioned after serving in the trenches in World War 1, army officer Henry Williamson moved to the village of Georgeham near Putsborough and sought solace in this peaceful and remote landscape. It inspired him to produce one of the classics of British nature writing, **Tarka the Otter**, using settings in north Devon and Exmoor to describe the life of the animal in poetic but unsentimental prose. Such is the book's enduring popularity that it continues to be used by the local tourism industry, including the Tarka Line railway and the 127km Tarka Trail – a long distance footpath which visits Croyde, Baggy Point and Woolacombe.

Follow the track over the open field and where the coast path veers right at a signpost keep straight ahead and then

along the left side of the field. With Croyde Bay now visible, go through a gate and along a narrow hedged thoroughfare. Ignore a tempting left turn and instead continue ahead on a wide track that after 1.4km veers south to wind its way downhill and eventually arrive at **Croyde**.

To visit the shops and cafés in the centre of the village turn left, otherwise cross over and turn right to walk alongside the road. Continue past the National Trust's Sandleigh Tea Room and Garden, then its car park, and out along the popular path beyond, with the low outline of Lundy island now visible 19km offshore. *The distinctive granite island outcrop of Lundy, which can be reached by boat from Bideford for day trips and overnight stays, boasts some wonderful wildlife and arguably England's remotest pub.*

At a choice of paths take the lower option to the left and follow it all the way out to **Baggy Point**. To your left, beyond Croyde Bay, is the estuary of the Rivers Taw and Torridge, downstream from Barnstaple and Bideford; and further round is the sharp outline of Hartland Point. At the tip of the headland walk back up the gentle flight of steps and at the top turn left for the path around the clifftop.

The **unusual white pole** on the clifftop beside the path is a former coastguard training post, also called a wreck post. It was built to resemble a ship's mast (the jagged edges of the pole are simply climbing steps) and was used to practise the breeches buoy life-saving technique. A rocket would have been fired towards the post and a line attached to the

▲ *Path out to Baggy Point*

top to allow the canvas breeches to act as a simple sling or harness so that a person called be winched from ship to shore via ropes. It was crude but effective and over the years saved the lives of hundreds of stricken sailors. The post on Baggy Point was restored in 2016 and is the last remaining pole on the north Devon coast.

Now there are sumptuous views northwards towards Morte Point, beyond Woolacombe, taking in the full length of Woolacombe Sands. Continue all the way along the obvious clifftop path until you reach the fenced drive down to Putsborough Sands. Turn left and follow this down through the car park and past the café to the beach. *Woolacombe and Croyde are surfing meccas where, as one local website puts it,* *an hour or so after low tide is your best bet at 'snagging a shady tube'.*

Now it's simply a question of walking the beautiful, wide, 4.8km sandy strip all the way back to Woolacombe – barefoot along the water's edge is a lovely option! (If the tide is particularly high or the weather inclement simply retrace your outward route through Woolacombe Warren.) When you get to a stream at the far end of the beach, almost at the buildings of Woolacombe, veer right towards the village to emerge by the Old Boathouse (the original lifeboat station); then either turn left for all the amenities in the centre of **Woolacombe** or turn right to return to the car park and the start of the walk.

Preparations for war

On the clifftop near Putsborough are the remains of a dummy pillbox, one of many built on Baggy Point between 1943 and 1944 as part of the training for troops preparing for the D-Day invasions. Because of its resemblance to the coastline of Normandy, the entire Woolacombe, Croyde and Braunton seaboard became the American army's Assault Training Centre (as it was called). It included mock-ups of ships' sides to practise embarkation on to landing craft, as well as minefields, craters, and metal anti-tank obstacles known as Czech hedgehogs. A large cork target in the bay was used for target practice by planes, as was Morte Point itself (and which permanently changed its outline). Thousands of troops rehearsed amphibious landings on Woolacombe Sand, sadly with some real casualties, and when suddenly they all sailed off one day in May 1944 local people knew that the invasion of Europe had begun. Over 3000 American soldiers died at Omaha Beach in Normandy and a local memorial to their sacrifice can be found off the Esplanade at Woolacombe.

Walk 9

Hartland Quay to Bude

Start	Hartland Quay (car park) SS 222 247
Finish	Bude (Summerleaze Beach) SS 205 065
Distance	23.5km (14.6 miles)
Total ascent	1335m (4380ft)
Time	8hr
Terrain	An undulating and unrelenting high-level cliff path, with steep drops and climbs through ten separate river valleys, including long flights of steps and rough surfaces
Map	OS Explorer 126/OS Landranger 190
Refreshments	Hartland Quay Hotel, seasonal cafés at Morwenstow and Sandymouth, plenty of choice at Bude
Public transport	Infrequent daily buses between Hartland Quay, Morwenstow and Bude, so plan your walk carefully
Parking	Hartland Quay and Bude (charge)

The origins of the South West Coast Path National Trail lie in the clifftop paths created by the coastguards and lookouts as they kept watch over the ungovernable seas; but north Cornwall's high, wild and often remote coastline has also attracted creative souls seeking freedom and expression. From poets and pacifists to eccentric vicars, the soaring cliffs south of Hartland Point have provided stimulation and escape – as they do for walkers now. As exhilarating as it is, however, you will also need to plan carefully as this is one of the most challenging sections of the entire England Coast Path, with numerous steep climbs and descents and little in the way of facilities. But, if you're fit, well prepared and the weather is kind, this is an absolutely cracking day's walk!

Leave the car park next to the hotel at Hartland Quay, located at the end of a narrow lane that drops rather alarmingly down the cliff slope towards the sea, and take the coast path southwards signposted Speke's Mill. Ahead are lines of stark jagged rocks and shattered cliffs. Immediately the path climbs up to the clifftop, but then drops down and kinks inland.

It must have taken some strength and ingenuity to build a safe mooring on this exposed and isolated coastline, especially back in the 1500s, but for several centuries **Hartland Quay** was busy with cargoes of limestone, slate and coal passing through. Although the quay itself had fallen into disrepair by 1900, its store buildings, stables and cottages were converted into a hotel and pub; but the location's sense of remoteness and detachment from the mainstream appeared to persist. As an interpretation board outside the hotel explains, a small side room of the pub was once called Hockins and Sons Bank and dealt in its own currency!

At **Speke's Mill Mouth**, where there is a waterfall that after rainfall is particularly dramatic, you can choose either the valley route or clifftop path (both signposted), although with plenty of lofty ascents ahead the former might be the better option this early on. *Far below are wave-cut platforms and reefs that*

◀ *Gull Rock near Marsland Mouth*

Map continues on page 80

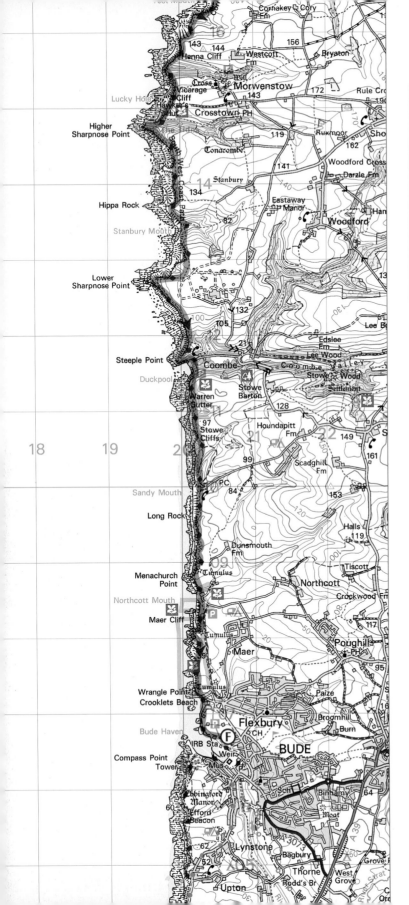

Ronnie's Hut at Marsland Mouth

extend out into the sea, while in the cliffs themselves the sedimentary rocks have been folded into remarkable shapes and layers.

The route soon resumes across the top of high, undulating cliffs with commanding sea views. If conditions are clear you should be able to see Lundy island to the north. After 3.5km, at **Mansley Cliff**, there is a turning for Elmscott Youth Hostel; then beyond this a short stretch along a country lane. Next to a small transmitter the path regains the edge of the huge cliffs, with exhilarating views up and down the coastline from **Nabor Point**. The picnic table on the open and exposed headland is well-sited, if rather windy.

Go carefully down to **Welcombe Mouth** and, via stepping stones, cross the stream, which falls on to the beach via a small waterfall. After climbing back up, the route then plunges down once more to **Marsland Mouth** via a long flight of steps – these steep and dramatic ups and downs set the pattern for this walk. However, pause at the top of the steps to visit **Ronnie's Hut**, the writing place of Ronald Duncan.

The coast path enters Cornwall ▶

Every day, writer **Ronald Duncan** (1914–1982) walked up to this small but comfortable hut near the top of the cliffs from his nearby home to enjoy solitude as well as inspiration. But there was a lot to this intriguing and complex man, described in the biographical note pinned up in his cabin as a poet, playwright, journalist, farmer and lover. Friends with such luminaries as Ezra Pound, TS Eliot and Henry Williamson, Duncan was a committed pacifist and founded a commune in this quiet coastal backwater during World War 2. Some of his poems are on display, including a couple about the local countryside; and there's even a contribution from Poet Laureate Simon Armitage, who composed a haiku in Duncan's honour when he passed through here on his own coastal walk in 2014.

At Marsland Mouth a sign welcomes you to Cornwall (Kernow), although a little oddly there's not one for walkers heading the other way into Devon. Now head back up to the top, only to drop back down via steps to cross Litter Mouth; then after **Henna Cliff** follow a broad zig zag track up on to **Vicarage Cliff**. By now the church tower of Morwenstow will be in sight inland, and this small village (less than 1km away) offers a pub and seasonal tearooms. This is roughly the midpoint of the walk, at 12.5km.

As you walk along the top of Vicarage Cliff look out for the National Trust sign for **Hawker's Hut**, the one-time refuge of local poet Reverend Robert Hawker. Made out of driftwood and timbers from shipwrecked vessels, it's situated just a few steps from the path and open to visitors.

The coast path now zig zags down to Tidna Chute (some of the natural features and locations along this coast have great names), then climbs up to **Higher Sharpnose Point**. As long as it's not too windy make sure to walk out along the narrow ridge to the end of the point for a superb viewpoint. There's an old stone building (a lookout station) that offers some shelter. *This rough and unforgiving section of coastline has claimed many ships and sailors over the years, with over 150 vessels lost on the rocks between Morwenstow and Bude alone.*

Continue along the obvious, well-waymarked clifftop path, then after 2km go down to cross a stream at **Stanbury Mouth**. Rather inevitably, plod the long way back up to the far side and on past a radar station with huge white satellite dishes.

Beyond **Lower Sharpnose Point** is a particularly exhilarating 1km section, where the path crests the high and undulating clifftop, culminating in the pinnacle of **Steeple Point**. Note the considerable cliff erosion that has taken place, and after wet weather in particular be careful close to the edge. At Sandymouth there is a café and toilets at the National Trust car park.

With 4km left to go, the route crosses the back of the pebbly beach at Sandymouth to follow the grassy path across the clifftop via **Northcott Mouth**. Go around the back of Crooklets Beach, past a row of beach huts and over Summerleaze Downs above Bude Sea Pool to finish at Summerleaze Beach in the popular and well-equipped seaside resort of **Bude**.

Song of the Western Men

Reverend Robert Hawker was the gloriously eccentric vicar of Morwenstow from 1835 to 1874. Today he's best known for his ballad *Song of the Western Men* (also known as *Trelawny*) which many consider Cornwall's unofficial anthem. The local landscape certainly fed his romantic and creative imagination, but he was also a diligent clergyman who was devoted to his local community and cared for shipwrecked sailors – many sadly washed up in his parish as corpses. He was by all accounts a tall, large man who habitually dressed in a fisherman's blue jersey and hessian sea boots, rather than the conventional vicar's outfit, and he smoked a pipe of Syrian tobacco. His voice was so commanding that it was said that he often stood outside his home and carried on a conversation with his neighbours at a farm across the valley! Cornwall County Council's excellent booklet guide to Hawker, including three circular walks, is available locally.

▲ *Lower Sharpnose Point from Steeple Point*

Banks of sea pink line the route from Stepper Point ▶

Padstow to Porthcothan

Start	Padstow (harbour) SW 919 754
Finish	Porthcothan SW 858 719
Distance	21.25km (13.2 miles)
Total ascent	575m (1890ft)
Time	5hr 30min
Terrain	Gently undulating clifftop, sandy bays, good paths throughout
Map	OS Explorer 104/OS Landranger 200
Refreshments	Plenty in Padstow, plus Trevone Beach Café, Trey Bay Café at Treyarnon and Porthcothan Bay Stores
Public transport	Frequent daily buses between Padstow and Porthcothan
Parking	Car parks in Padstow (charge)

This relatively straightforward but nevertheless lovely walk involves a prominent river estuary, two fine headlands and eight accessible sandy beaches, not to mention blow holes and a lighthouse – in other words, all the ingredients for the perfect outing on the England Coast Path in the south west. Even better, a handy and regular bus connection allows a car-free approach, with the bus also calling at Treyarnon, Constantine and Harlyn bays if you want a shorter option. Depending on the season, I'd recommend packing a small towel and perhaps swimwear as the temptation to either take a dip, or at the very least a paddle to cool hot feet, might be irresistible at the end of the walk.

Leave the north side of the harbour at Padstow, taking the path uphill on the left signposted coast path to Hawkers Cove. Follow the well-walked route out to the war memorial at St Saviour's Point and on along the low cliffs, with rewarding views back over Padstow and across the whole of the Camel Estuary.

In geological terms the **Camel Estuary**, which extends for 8km inland towards Wadebridge, is a ria or deep river valley drowned by rising sea levels following a period of glaciation. At Padstow it widens to almost 1.2km and the scene, as you look down from the coast path above the town, is usually one of yachts and small boats going about their business, including the regular Black Tor ferry from Padstow across to Rock. The sandbanks at the estuary mouth have long been a hazard for shipping, including the notorious Doom Bar which supposedly got its name when a local man had an ill-fated encounter with a mermaid. These days it's more likely to be associated with a popular amber ale from Sharp's Brewery of Cornwall.

Rounding **Harbour Cove** the path keeps to the field edge at the back of the dunes, or you can follow the edge of the beach. After **Hawker's Cove**, with its seasonal tea garden, the cliffs begin to rise and after 4.5km from the start of the walk you arrive at Stepper Point overlooking the mouth of the estuary. Rounding the headland, keep to the signposted path to reach the distinctive daymark, a solid stone tower built as a navigational aid for seafarers.

The walk now takes on a different perspective as you follow the high cliffs south westwards, with wonderful views of Trevose Head opening out before you. Although there are a few slopes the gradients are generally easy and the clifftop is wide and accommodating. Go round the gaping edge of **Pepper Hole** and on via **Gunver Head** towards Trevone Bay. The path skirts a remarkable circular chasm in the grassy clifftop, called **Round Hole**, before dropping down to cross the sand at the back of **Trevone Bay**.

There are in fact two of these spectacular natural chasms, both called **Round Hole**, on this walk. Sometimes known as a blow hole or sink hole, they are inland sea caves that have collapsed following constant pounding by the waves. The one before you at Trevone is 25m deep and resembles a huge crater, as if a meteor has struck! If you peer over the edge you can see the sea washing in and out far below, while at other locations on the cliff path you can hear the

booming sound of the waves crashing into other caves hidden beneath your feet. It can be an eerie and sometimes rather disconcerting sound.

The fenced path resumes above the low, rocky shoreline and rounds more cliffs before arriving at **Harlyn Bay**, a beautiful stretch of pristine sand as golden in colour as Cornish clotted cream. Walk along the sheltered beach, popular with families, for approximately 340 metres before taking the steps up to the clifftop. The coast path resumes its obvious and easy route, now around **Mother Ivey's Bay**, and via clifftop villas and a lifeboat station perched on stilts above the waves. *In 1967*

Padstow lifeboat station was re-sited here from Hawker's Cove after silting in the mouth of the Camel Estuary rendered the original base inoperable.

The route now swings west to the far tip of **Trevose Head**, 3.6km beyond Harlyn. This is a wilder and more remote section of coastline with gorse and rougher open slopes. Keep to the lower waymarked path and aim for the lighthouse, afterwards crossing its road to drop down past the site of an old quarry to **Dinas Head** on the western edge of the headland. *From the splendid promontory of Dinas Head there are far-ranging views south westwards along the Cornwall coast as far as St Ives and Pendeen Watch (Walk 11).*

conditions. Although there are well-known surfing meccas like Fistral Beach at Newquay, which hosts world championships, other beaches at Polzeath, Sennen and Perranporth are equally impressive. On this walk, the beaches tend to be smaller but the surfing and bodyboarding is no less spectacular and enjoyable. Depending on the season, surf schools are often busy giving lessons and RNLI lifeguards patrol Trevone, Harlyn, Constantine, Treyarnon and Porthtowan beaches.

Beyond the low rocky promontory of **Treyarnon Point** is the little gem of Treyarnon Bay, overlooked by a youth hostel. *Located just 50 metres from the sea, YHA Treyarnon Bay is a perfect base for exploring the coast, plus the adjoining Trey Bay Café is highly recommended.*

After **Treyarnon Bay** the cliffs rise again and the path weaves its way along the top, turning this way and that past a series of tiny coves and various small islands, stacks and weathered cliffs. Finally the trail swings inland and makes its way down to **Porthcothan**. Cross the road bridge to reach the bus stop or car park by the beach shop.

Attention all shipping

Trevose is one of Cornwall's most prominent and visible headlands with cliffs rising 45m above the waves. Trinity House first built a lighthouse here in 1847 to aid vessels heading in and out of the Bristol Channel, but frequent sea mists tended to obscure the light and vessels continued to founder. So in 1911 a fog horn was erected, but not just any old fog horn. Specially designed by Lord Rayleigh, scientific advisor to Trinity House at the time, it was hexagonal in length and almost 12 metres long and was said to look like an enormous trumpet. It could be heard over 13km away and was one of the largest foghorns ever used. The coast path passes next to the lighthouse, so if it happens to be a misty day when you walk past just count yourself lucky that the foghorn was decommissioned in 1963.

The route descends the gently sloping and open clifftop to **Booby's Bay**, past the second Round Hole of the day. At low tide the sandy beach extends into **Constantine Bay** and you can walk safely across the entire expanse; otherwise follow the path around the back of the beach.

At beaches and bays all along the Cornwall coast you will see people **surfing** throughout the year, including in the winter months (albeit in wetsuits). Cornwall's position sticking out into the Atlantic usually guarantees a good sea swell, plus there's a choice of numerous and highly attractive beaches where reefs and currents produce different

Pendeen to Penzance

Start	Pendeen (main street) SW 383 343
Finish	Penzance (bus station) SW 476 305
Distance	45.5km (28.3 miles)
Total ascent	1100m (3610ft)
Time	13hr
Terrain	Undulating cliff path with some steep ascents and descents, as well as sandy and stony beaches. Beyond Lamorna the path is rocky and narrow and can get overgrown in summer.
Map	OS Explorer 102/OS Landranger 203
Refreshments	At numerous locations, including Geevor Tin Mine, Sennen Cove, Land's End, Porthcurno, Lamorna and Mousehole
Public transport	Daily bus service from Penzance serves all main points on route, including Pendeen, Sennen Cove, Porthcurno and Mousehole
Parking	Roadside at Pendeen, car parks at Porthcurno and Penzance (both charge)
Note	This 2-day walk covers Pendeen to Porthcurno (25.75km/16 miles) then Porthcurno to Penzance (18.5km/11.5 miles); or if you want to omit the urban ending finish the walk at Mousehole (Pendeen to Sennen Cove, 16.25km/10.1 miles, Sennen Cove to Mousehole, 22.75km/14.1 miles)

Gwennap Head

This invigorating 2-day walk offers so much, from towering cliffs with lighthouses and lookout stations to sweeping golden bays and tiny hidden coves. Be the first and last in England as you walk round the Land's End peninsula; but also immerse yourself in Cornish culture – from choughs and cream teas to surfers, fishing and the legacy of tin mining. The path is open and exposed in places and your leg muscles will get a workout, but there is so much to see that building time into your schedule to linger and explore is recommended. Better still, a decent daily bus service meets all the key points on the walk, so you can adapt distances and destinations to suit and effectively walk around England's south west tip from a base like Penzance.

Day 1

Starting from the bus stop in the centre of Pendeen, follow the lane signposted Pendeen Lighthouse out to the coast path, turning left on to the National Trail opposite cottages before you reach Pendeen Watch and its low-set, handsome lighthouse. Within a few minutes you are walking through a rather untidy, despoiled landscape of ruined buildings, chimneys and assorted mounds that are the remains of a once thriving mining industry.

The **Cornish Mining World Heritage Site** today echoes to the footfall of visitors rather than the clank of machinery and the sight and smell of dozens of smoking chimneys, but this was once the epicentre of the world's metal mining. Throughout the 18th and 19th centuries, Cornwall was a leading producer of tin and copper, with engineering advances such as revolutionary new steam engines that allowed for deeper and more productive mining, including far out under the sea bed. Geevor Tin Mine (museum,

The Crowns engine houses at Botallack (photo: Chiz Dakin)

underground tours, café, toilets) is just a five-minute walk from the path and a visit is recommended. This was the last Cornish tin mine to close, in 1990, but was subsequently turned into an excellent industrial heritage centre – by some of the same men that once toiled deep below the surface.

The route continues past the former arsenic works of Levant Mine and Botallack Mine. On the cliffside far below are the shells of two engine houses known as **The Crowns**, probably the most photographed mining relics on the coast. Far more ancient is the enigmatic site of Kenidjack Cliff Castle, an Iron Age promontory fort on the cliffs high above.

After 5km you reach **Cape Cornwall**, a fine mini headland topped by an old mining tower. The short there-and-back diversion is a must, not least for the fine views from England's only named cape, including towards some offshore rocks known as The Brisons, whose distinctive outline is said to resemble General de Gaulle lying in a bath. *Cape Cornwall was so-named because medieval cartographers thought that it was the most westerly point of the English mainland, only to discover later that Land's End was further out.*

Resume the clifftop trail past the chambered cairn of Carn Gluse, followed by a descent into the **Cot Valley**. Beyond Gribba Point the huge golden sweep of **Whitesand Bay** comes into view as the path drops down gradually towards the shore. Reaching the water's edge after a long clifftop section may prove irresistible, so if the tide permits you can enjoy a 2km route across the sand to Sennen Cove, otherwise the path is at the back of the beach.

Sennen Cove is popular with surfers and sunbathers and there are numerous cafés and other facilities. The waymarked trail continues across the clifftop beyond the lifeboat station and soon reaches **Land's End**. Thread your way through the crowds milling around the visitor complex, including the First and Last House and the famous signpost pointing to John o' Groats, and on along the broad clifftop on any one of numerous small paths. *In view offshore is Longships lighthouse, perched on a small reef, while 40km further out and visible on a clear day are the Scilly Isles.*

The undulating path across the open clifftop is easy to follow and the views are fantastic. A succession of headlands reveal sheer cliffs and small coves far below and it's worth

Nanjizal, between Land's End and Gwennap Head

Map continues on page 94

looking out for seals and cetaceans, since the seas off Cornwall are often vibrant with marine life.

This is a wonderful section of path that is comparatively wild and remote. There are no cafés or car parks, nor indeed much human habitation at all, just a breath-taking clifftop path and an awful lot of untamed sea. Then, 6km after leaving Land's End, you arrive at the signal station at **Gwennap Head**. The trail now dips down to the small bay of Porthgwarra and then on to the beautiful sandy cove of **Porthcurno** (café and toilets in both). Just before the latter is the **Minack Theatre**, an elegant amphitheatre cut into the rocks of the cliffs in the 1930s and which still holds open-air productions.

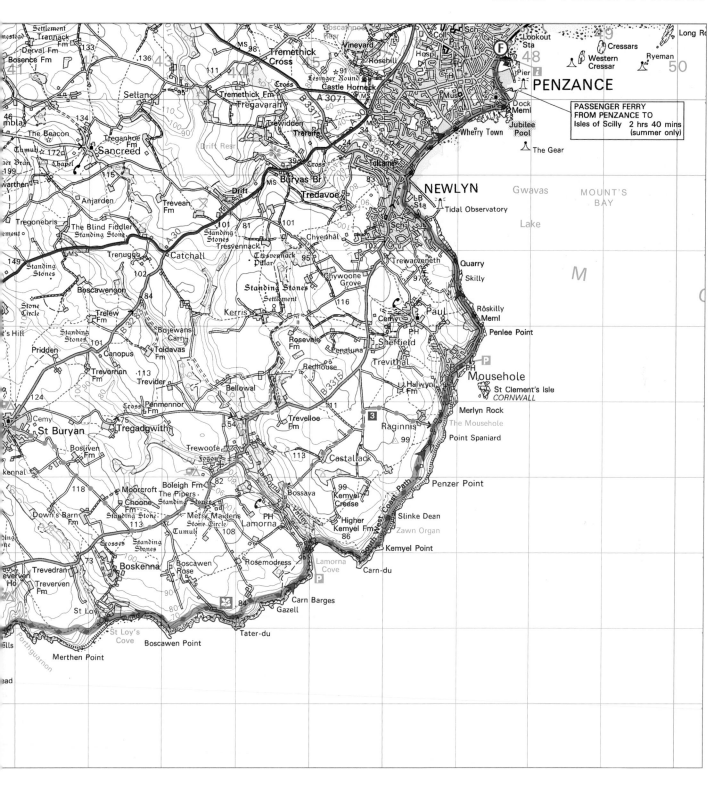

The neat sandy cove at **Porthcurno**, framed by high cliffs and in summer a shimmering turquoise sea, is an exquisite location; and the bus bravely ventures all the way down the narrow lane to the beach car park at the foot of the strung-out village. But Porthcurno's greater claim to fame is as an historic communications centre, since one of the first ocean cables from overseas came ashore here (all the way from Bombay, laid in 1870). For a while, Porthcurno Telegraph Station assumed a worldwide importance, with Cable and Wireless establishing a training college nearby. Around the time of the two World Wars Porthcurno became one of the largest submarine cable stations in the world. There's more about all this in a fascinating village museum called PK Porthcurno.

Day 2

The trail now becomes rougher underfoot, with a steep ascent from the tiny **Penberth Cove**, where fishing boats are pulled up on the slipway. At **St Loy** the path wanders past some lush but sheltered wooded gardens, almost tropical in nature with bamboo and palms; then after this it takes to the rocky beach for 200 metres before returning to the clifftop.

There's a handy café and toilets at **Lamorna Cove**, but after this the uneven path and encroaching vegetation makes for slower progress. With great views across Mount's Bay to the island castle of St Michael's Mount, the well-waymarked route eventually takes to tarmac and drops down into the popular village of **Mousehole** with plenty of facilities.

Walk the broad pavement of the coast road towards **Newlyn**, a working fishing port with a harbour full of seagoing trawlers; then join the long promenade into **Penzance**. *Seawards is Jubilee Pool, the town's celebrated Art Deco sea water and geothermally heated pool that's still popular today (café open to non-swimmers).*

Cornwall and its choughs

Few birds can have such a close association with an individual county as the chough does with Cornwall. It resembles a small crow, but with a red bill and red legs, and is at home on cliffs and coastal slopes. The chough features on Cornwall's coat of arms, alongside a miner and a fisherman, and is so rooted in Cornish culture that, according to legend, King Arthur changed into a chough when he died, with red feet and beak signifying his bloody end. Unfortunately, persistent hunting and a loss of coastal feeding habitat (traditional grazing pasture) effectively wiped them out by the 1940s, as it did throughout England. However, since 2001 a pioneering conservation project has helped this iconic bird return to the Cornish coast, with now over 100 breeding pairs. Listen and look out for them on this walk, but observe local signs and keep dogs under close control in the breeding season (March to July).

The Lizard

Start/Finish	Lizard (village centre car park) SW 703 125
Distance	14km (8.7 miles)
Total ascent	330m (1080ft)
Time	3hr 30min
Terrain	Mostly straightforward clifftop paths with just a few slopes, some lanes and open heath
Map	OS Explorer 103/OS Landranger 203
Refreshments	Cafés and pubs at Lizard, Lizard Point (Wavecrest Café) and Cadgwith (Old Cellars), seasonal café at Kynance Cove
Public transport	Daily buses to Lizard from Helston
Parking	Lizard (on green in village centre)

The most southerly point on the British mainland doesn't have the razzamatazz of Land's End, which is probably a good thing. Instead, the Lizard peninsula, effectively a high and open plateau of heath and farmland, feels nicely remote. There's not much to the namesake village beyond the shops around the central green, but its richness is in its unique geology, plants and wildlife; and it's on the cliff path that the Lizard is at its most majestic, with bands of coloured rock and slopes full of wildflowers. This is a moderate walk in terms of difficulty, but high for points of interest. Off the peninsula the English Channel and Atlantic Ocean meet to battle it out; and this was also where the Spanish Armada was first sighted on 29 July 1588. Ship ahoy!

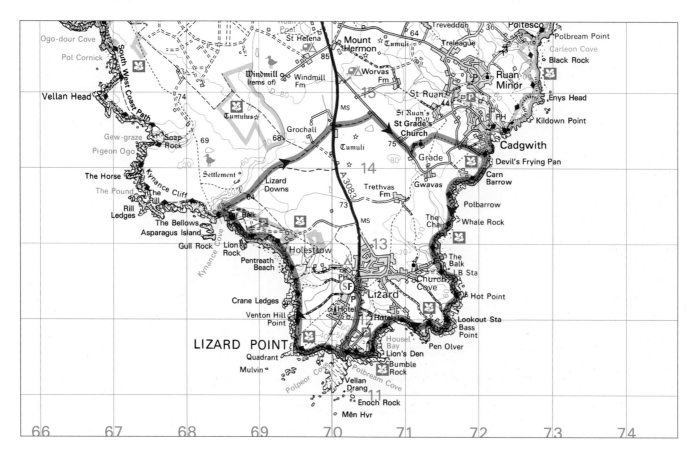

From the centre of Lizard village follow the off-road path down to Lizard Point and turn right by the Wavecrest Café. A well-walked and very straightforward 3.5km cliff path heads all the way along to **Kynance Cove**, via a succession of low, brooding headlands interspersed by exciting, rocky coves where seals can sometimes be spotted. *The Lizard is especially famous for serpentine, a smooth metamorphic rock which here at Kynance Cove appears as wavy bands of shiny dark green and red, a bit like a reptile's skin.*

The tidal beach at **Kynance Cove**, with its pristine golden sand and turquoise water, is very popular with holidaymakers and there's a seasonal café and toilets. There are in fact several small coves ringed with rock stacks and caves, including the Devil's Letterbox where the swell causes a powerful suction of air through a crack in the rocks above.

Follow the vehicle track up the narrow valley behind the café ('kynance' is from the Cornish kewnans, meaning ravine)

England's most southerly road sign (photo: Chiz Pakin)

Perhaps not unexpectedly, Britain's most southerly location enjoys a mild, maritime climate that, coupled with its distinctive geology and range of habitats, gives rise to a rich natural history. **The Lizard National Nature Reserve** covers the cliffs and coastal slopes where orchids, sea thrift, campions and wild chives all grow; while the heathland of Lizard Downs contains dwarf rush and wild asparagus, as well as the vibrant colours of flowering gorse in the summer. Here you may come across an adder basking in the sun, as well as dragonflies and beetles that are attracted to the small ponds. On the coast be alert for resident choughs, peregrines and ravens.

and all way back up to the clifftop. Where it heads over to the large car park on the right branch half-left, at a blue public bridleway marker, and follow this clear route north-eastwards across the middle of a wide area of heathland called **Lizard Downs**.

After 2km of peaceful walking you come to a road on the far side of the heath. Cross over and continue on the track opposite that eventually meets a quiet lane. Turn right and follow this, going straight on at a junction, then left for a gated path to the isolated **St Grade's Church**.

▲ *Cadgwith Cove Crab shop*

Continue along the field edge beyond, swinging right at the end for a path that meets a lane at a junction. Go diagonally left and then right, on a vehicle track past buildings, signposted Inglewidden. Follow this as it swings left and drops down into the picture-perfect fishing village of **Cadgwith**.

Apart from the café and pub, the immediate attraction of Cadgwith is the beachside **Cadgwith Cove Crab** shop that sells fresh local produce, including lobster wraps and home-made prawn sandwiches. Fishing boats, winched high up the shingle, go out daily. Until the 1950s this would have been for pilchards, which were once caught in vast numbers, but over-fishing caused the shoals to disappear and now the catch is shellfish, like brown and spider crabs, as well as mackerel, shark and mullet. Around the cove are various trappings from this long established industry, including gear lofts, capstan houses and pilchard cellars, some of which have recently been purchased by the Cadgwith Fishing Cove Trust in order to preserve the village's heritage and provide today's local fishermen with storage.

Retrace your steps back up to the clifftop then turn left, on the South West Coast Path, at the signpost for the **Devil's Frying Pan**. *The 60m chasm in the cliffs, with an arched entrance to the sea, is known as the Devil's Frying Pan and was caused by the roof of a sea cave collapsing.*

Continue on the clifftop path for 3.2km until you reach Lizard lifeboat station on the far side of **Church Cove**. The boat is launched from the foot of the 45m cliffs. Further on is the National Coastwatch Institution **lookout station** at Bass Point,

with memorials beside the path to several notable shipwrecks. After this you come to **Housel Bay**, with its clifftop hotel overlooking the cove.

Approaching the tip of the peninsula, the cliff path continues past the prominent twin towers of Lizard lighthouse. There has been a light here for over 250 years and part of the building is now a heritage centre run by Trinity House.

Unlike Land's End, at Lizard Point you can safely venture down to the shoreline at the foot of the cliffs by following the easy, looping track below the souvenir shops. Now, truly, you can say you are the southernmost person on the British mainland.

To return to the start of the walk simply retrace your steps for the off-road path back to **Lizard** village, where there is a range of shops and cafés, including locally-made Cornish pasties.

Cornish pasties have been around for centuries, traditionally a staple food of poorer working families as they were an easy-to-eat convenience food that fitted neatly in a pocket. It's said that the pasty's distinctive crimped edge was used as a discardable handle by tin miners because of high levels of arsenic in many mines that tainted their fingers. The traditional recipe should include diced or minced beef, plus swede, onion and diced or sliced potato, with a light seasoning. It's been awarded protected status by the EU and latterly the British government, meaning that only pasties made in Cornwall from a traditional recipe can be called Cornish pasties. For an authentic, locally made pasty check out Ann's Pasties, based in Porthleven near Helston and with a shop in Lizard village.

Coastal extremities

By rights, Lizard Point should be every bit as well known as Land's End. Sure, Land's End is the most westerly location on the English mainland (Ardnamurchan Point holds that title for the British mainland), but it's on the Lizard that you are the furthest south that you can be. The ultimate south–north British walking journey, which some have undertaken, is Lizard Point to Dunnet Head, near Thurso, since it's the latter rather than nearby John o' Groats that's the northernmost point on the British mainland. Despite this, the journey between Land's End and John o' Groats – the two extreme points – is the one that over the years has caught people's imagination rather than the more prosaic points on a compass or lines of latitude. Still, with Lowestoft Ness in Suffolk being England's easternmost point, perhaps the England Coast Path is laying down another walking challenge to join the geographical extremes?

▶ *Lizard Lighthouse is now a heritage centre run by Trinity House (photo: Chiz Dakin)*

Portscatho and the Roseland Peninsula

Start/Finish	Portscatho (main square) SW 876 352
Distance	15.75km (9.8 miles)
Total ascent	290m (950ft)
Time	4hr
Terrain	Country lanes, wooded paths, wide and straightforward clifftop tracks
Map	OS Explorer 105/OS Landranger 204
Refreshments	Boathouse Café and Plume of Feathers pub at Portscatho, Porth Tea Room near Towan Beach
Public transport	Daily buses to Gerrans and Portscatho from Truro
Parking	Visitor car parks at Portscatho (charge)

Cornwall's comparatively secluded and nature-rich Roseland Peninsula lies to the east of the River Fal, and with its lush vegetation, quiet paths and mild climate it's a rewarding place to explore on foot. The coast path is mostly easy and straightforward and hugs the shoreline, which varies from densely wooded inlets to open clifftop. The latter is crowned by St Anthony Head, once an important military lookout point, since it enjoys sweeping views from the Lizard all the way across Falmouth Bay and into Carrick Roads. It's one of those lofty vantage points where you can idle away an hour in the sunshine simply gazing at all the nautical activity on the water below; or, perhaps equally rewarding, keeping a lookout out for passing dolphins, seals and even basking sharks in the summer months.

From the square in the centre of Portscatho, where the pub, shop and café are all located, walk up the steep road (called Higher Town) to the adjoining community of Gerrans. Turn left opposite the **church** along Treloan Lane, next to the Royal Standard pub. *Gerrans Parish Heritage Centre, with plenty of information about local history, is just around the corner by the village green (open weekday afternoons in the main holiday season).*

In common with much of Cornwall's rocky and unforgiving coast, there have been plenty of shipwrecks around the **Roseland Peninsula** and many of the local barns, cottages and even Gerrans church contain timbers from ships that have foundered. Despite some heroic rescues, many lives have been lost. For instance, 19 out of a crew of 23 from a German cargo ship called *Hera* perished when it went down in 1914 after hitting Gull Rock on the far side of Gerrans Bay. Fifteen of the victims were subsequently buried in St Veryan churchyard on Roseland. Remarkably, though, they were all buried in a single grave, head to toe, that stretches 30 metres and is believed to be the longest of its kind in the UK. The names of all the sailors are commemorated and hundreds of people turned out at this small parish church to mark the centenary of the tragedy.

Follow the lane past a campsite to the very end, which then continues as a public bridleway and unmade track that after 3km eventually

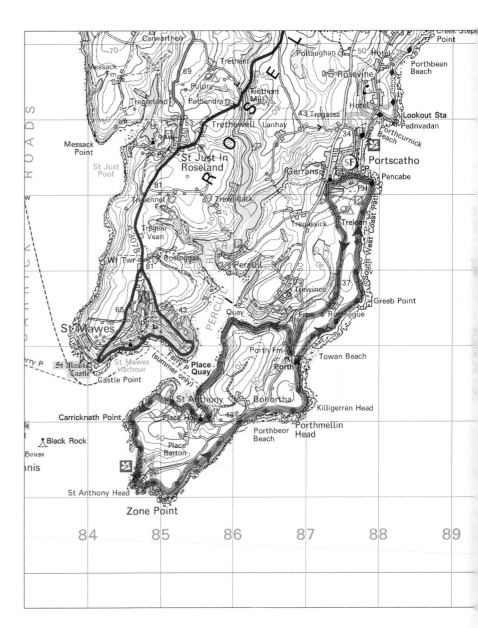

emerges on to a country road. Turn left on to this to reach the National Trust car park, café and toilets at **Porth**.

Just before the car park turn right and go down past the farm on a path into woodland, signposted Place Quay. The National Trust's popular permissive route skirts the thickly wooded peninsula, with impressive views across the mouth of the Percuil River to St Mawes. Beyond **Place Quay** walk up the lane next to **Place House**, then at the South West Coast Path signpost turn right to walk past St Anthony's Church and the back of the imposing house. *A regular foot ferry operates daily between Place Quay and St Mawes (April to October), with the 10-minute crossing allowing you to pop across the water and back for lunch!*

St Anthony's Church was established in the Middle Ages by Augustinian monks from Plympton in Devon. It fell into disrepair but, in the 19th century, was restored by Samuel Spry, MP for Bodmin, and the turreted Place House next door remains the Spry family's ancestral home. The church has a striking carved roof and there are numerous monuments to family members, including Rear Admiral Sir Richard Spry who died in 1775. The overgrown churchyard outside is equally interesting and atmospheric, with the coast path making its way past long-abandoned gravestones and even a medieval coffin unearthed during the renovation in 1850. Today the church is maintained by the Churches Conservation Trust and is open to visitors most of the year.

Continue through woods and over fields on a well-sign-posted route to reach the shoreline opposite St Mawes. With expanding views across Falmouth Bay, carry on along low cliffs with pine-topped promontories and small sandy coves. Go past a curious little stone building, which turns out to be the former paraffin store for the lighthouse, and stay on the path until just before the lighthouse itself. *The lighthouse was built to warn ships about a treacherous offshore reef, but more recently it's been used in the opening credits of the children's TV series Fraggle Rock.*

The route now doubles back and climbs steeply up to the car park, toilets and remains of the fortifications and lookout position that cluster on the tip of **St Anthony Head**.

From St Anthony Head you can begin to appreciate the vast size of the **Fal Estuary**, with Carrick Roads providing safe and sheltered anchorage. Falmouth has a rich maritime heritage stretching back hundreds of years and it was here, on Pendennis Point, that Henry VIII built a powerful fortress to protect the country from invasion from France and later Spain. Pendennis Castle went on to see service during the Civil War, the Napoleonic Wars and even as recently as the two World Wars. Guarding the opposite headland is St Mawes Castle, also built by King Henry, but as a smaller artillery fort and designed in a distinctive clover shape. Both castles are cared for by English Heritage and are open to the public.

▲ *Lighthouse at St Anthony Head*

Porthbeor Beach on the eastern side of the Roseland peninsula

The remaining 7km back to Portscatho is along an easy and scenic clifftop trail with only a few modest undulations. Follow the path via **Zone Point** and cross Drake's Downs to reach **Porthmellin Head**. At **Towan Beach** you can make a small diversion inland to visit the café at Porth, which you passed earlier in the walk. There are a few places where you can get down to the shoreline itself and at low tide narrow strips of sand are revealed.

The coast path continues to **Greeb Point** where there are glorious views across Gerrans Bay to Nare Head, with Gull Rock just offshore; and beyond that Dodman Point. Eventually you reach the houses of **Portscatho** and join a short lane that comes out at the square in the centre of the former fishing village. *The warm and damp maritime climate means Roseland is rich in wild plants and flowers, from bluebells and primroses in April through to thrift, sea campion and wild thyme in the early summer.*

Keeping watch on the headland

Given the importance of the Fal Estuary and Carrick Roads, the open and elevated tip of the Roseland Peninsula has always been of strategic importance. Yachts, trawlers and tankers might grab the attention today, but in the past eyes were peeled for hostile invaders. A gun battery and observation point were established on the headland in Napoleonic times and significantly strengthened during the two World Wars. Lookouts were posted to identify enemy ships, then calculate their positions and relay the information to nearby gunners, and many of the buildings and gun emplacements from that time remain. Happily it's a more peaceful scene today, and apart from the busy nautical activity there is also a rich marine life off the south Cornwall coast. Atlantic grey seals and bottlenose dolphins can be seen throughout the year, but in summer also look out for basking sharks feeding on plankton off the headland.

▶ *Prawle Point from Langerstone Point (photo: Chiz Dakin)*

Walk 14

Prawle Point and Start Point

Start/Finish	Beesands (beach car park) SX 819 405
Distance	23km (14.3 miles)
Total ascent	650m (2130ft)
Time	6hr
Terrain	Country lanes, field tracks, cliff paths that are rocky and in places steep
Map	OS OL20/OS Landranger 202
Refreshments	Cricket Inn and Britannia@TheBeach at Beesands, pub and café at East Prawle
Public transport	None
Parking	Car park by beach at Beesands

The England Coast Path is punctuated by a series of mighty peninsulas and headlands, including St Bees, Flamborough and the Lizard, all featured elsewhere in this book. Devon's big hitters are Prawle Point and Start Point, and this walk takes in both on an energetic and varied route that also includes a succession of delightful coves and beaches with opportunities for a dip if conditions are suitable. Prawle Point is the county's southernmost tip and naturally enough the views across the waters are sweeping and far-reaching. They're also monitored by the clifftop lookout station, next to which is a fascinating information point and handy shelter if the weather is particularly bracing. This is an exciting and occasionally demanding wind-in-the-hair journey along one of England's top cliff paths.

Walk south along the shore road at Beesands past the Cricket Inn and row of cottages for the clifftop route across **Tinsey Head**. In 2km you reach **Hallsands**, where the waymarked coast path briefly passes behind buildings to return to the cliff edge and a viewing platform overlooking the old village abandoned in 1917.

Although a small settlement still exists at **Hallsands**, a century ago the original village could be found perched on a rocky shelf below the cliffs at this point. However, one night in January 1917 a combination of fierce storm and high tide washed away 29 homes and destroyed the small community. In fact, the root of the disaster lay out in the bay where

▲ *All that remains of the old village of Hallsands, before its watery end*

for several years shingle and sand had been dredged as part of work to extend the naval dockyard at Plymouth. This in effect removed a protective offshore ridge and left the village open to the full blast of the sea. Luckily all the villagers survived, but they were forced to leave Hallsands for good and a cover-up at a subsequent inquiry cheated them of any compensation. A few forlorn buildings at the foot of the cliffs are all that remain.

Now head away from the sea on a narrow lane that climbs steadily uphill. Go left at the very top and then straight over at a junction (signposted Lannacombe). Drop down to the valley bottom, then take the second turning on the left on another quiet lane. Beyond a house go left on a rising bridleway signposted East Prawle.

The route climbs out of the trees and up and across the steeply sloping open hillside. When it levels out there's an excellent vista of both inland Devon and out to sea. Follow this clear and well-waymarked bridleway along the hilltop and around **Higher Borough** and **Woodcombe** farms until after 5.8km you reach **East Prawle**. *The Pigs Nose at East Prawle has variously*

been a smugglers' haunt, Victorian hotel and 1950s petrol station, but now it's a popular village pub with good food and drink.

Go left into the centre of the village and up to the green where the pub and nearby Piglet Stores and Café are located. Turn left in front of the public toilets to take the lane indicated Prawle Point. At the second bend go straight on along a bridleway and at the end turn left for a hedged path down to reach the coast path near **Gammon Head**.

Drop down to the lower cliff path and turn left to follow this high above exquisite sandy coves. Bolt Head and Salcombe

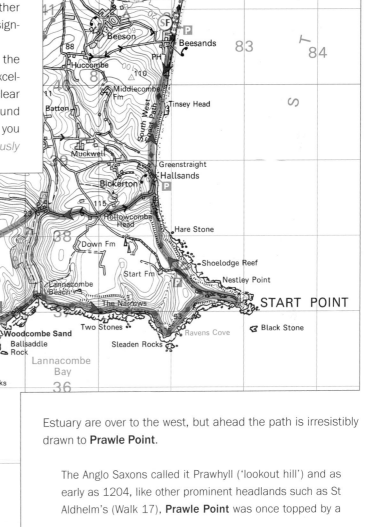

Estuary are over to the west, but ahead the path is irresistibly drawn to **Prawle Point**.

The Anglo Saxons called it Prawhyll ('lookout hill') and as early as 1204, like other prominent headlands such as St Aldhelm's (Walk 17), **Prawle Point** was once topped by a

medieval chapel. Inevitably such a southerly location is a well-known staging point for migrating wildlife, including butterflies like red admirals and painted ladies that can sometimes drift over the Channel on warm continental winds in large numbers. There's plenty of birdlife, too, including all the coastal birds that you would expect, although Prawle is also important for the nationally rare if rather unshowy cirl bunting, a small brown field bird which feeds on the seeds of arable weeds. Wheatears, stonechats and rock pipits can also be found along the coast, as well as the occasional peregrine falcon.

Once you've taken in the views and inspected the excellent visitor centre in the building next to the **lookout station**, continue eastwards towards Start Point, 8km further along the coast path. It begins by dropping down to the lower but still rocky shoreline, where wave-cut platforms extend out into the sea. As the path becomes rougher underfoot, ignore a side turning to Woodcombe Sand and stay on the main path. You can easily access the small beach at **Lannacombe** for a paddle if conditions allow, after which the path hugs the clifftop above sheltered coves and climbs up to the airy ridge that leads to the tip of **Start Point**.

Now the whole of Start Bay is suddenly and spectacularly revealed at your feet, stretching all the way round to Dartmouth and Kingswear. A signpost indicates that Poole is 168 miles (270km) and Minehead 462 miles (743km) away via the South West Coast Path.

When **Start Point lighthouse** began flashing its warning to shipping in 1836 the notorious offshore rocks and reefs had already claimed a large number of vessels. An extensive and shifting sandbank known as The Skerries extends off the point in a north easterly direction and at low water is very close to the surface, as well as affecting the wave patterns and swell in the bay. Meanwhile, in sight just off the headland is Black Stone, a small lump of rock that on its own has accounted for a number of ships. In a ferocious blizzard on 9 March 1891 a steamer struck Black Stone and sank, then a sailing ship and two schooners were also driven on to the rocks at Start Point. In just 24 hours a total of 52 people drowned.

It would seem churlish not to walk down the deserted road for the short distance to the lighthouse at the very end of the point. After this turn round and follow it back up to the grassy car park and viewpoint at the very top of the cliffs, then branch off to the right on the coast path that drops gradually down into Hallsands. Retrace your steps across Tinsey Head to return to **Beesands**. *Keith Richards of the Rolling Stones spent childhood holidays at Beesands and it is rumoured that he and Mick Jagger first performed in public at the Cricket Inn in the village.*

NCI – 'eyes along the coast'

The lookout station on Prawle Point is one of 57 around the coast of England and Wales operated by the National Coastwatch Institution (NCI). The organisation plays a vital role supporting HM Coastguard by monitoring the shipping around our frequently hazardous shores, and nowhere can it be more treacherous than the so-called 'ship trap' off Prawle and Start Points. The visitor centre on the headland lists some of the vessels that have come to grief; but it also shows how activity on the water is tracked today. As well as looking through a high-powered telescope, you can study a radar monitor showing the real-time position of offshore craft – there are more out there than you probably realise. NCI watchkeepers, who are all volunteers, also keep a beady eye on other coast users, including walkers, and can be the first to raise the alarm when misfortunes occur, so remember to say hello to them and perhaps make a donation while you're passing.

Walk 15

Beer and Branscombe

Start/Finish	Beer (beach slipway) SY 229 891
Distance	9.75km (6 miles)
Total ascent	405m (1330ft)
Time	3hr
Terrain	Field paths and tracks, pavement, cliff path that is occasionally steep and towards the end rough underfoot
Map	OS Explorer 115 & 116/OS Landranger 192
Refreshments	Pubs and cafés in Beer, including on the beach, Sea Shanty Beach Café at Branscombe Beach
Public transport	Daily buses from Seaton, Sidmouth and Lyme Regis
Parking	Cliff Top car park (charge)

As elsewhere around the English coast, there's been a long tradition of smuggling, wrecking and scavenging on Devon's shores. In the 18th and 19th centuries, vast amounts of illicit brandy, tobacco and tea were brought ashore in secret to avoid the attention of the customs men. Local figures like Jack Rattenbury from Beer made it an artform, hiding contraband in caves in the cliffs and sinking barrels of brandy in the shallows (corks attached by string to the barrels marked their locations – it was known as 'sowing the crop'). All kinds of flotsam could be found on the shore and people naturally profited. Fast forward to 2007 and washed-up booty from a container ship on Branscombe Beach drew huge crowds eager for what they could find. Lawless looters or opportunist treasure-seekers? This is a relatively short but highly scenic walk, with a rough section towards the end that can be avoided if need be.

From the top of the slipway at Beer beach, opposite the Anchor Inn, walk up the main street (Fore Street) past the shops, with streams running down open gutters either side. Follow it as it swings left and leaves the shops behind, then at a sharp bend go straight on, signposted Branscombe. Turn left on to Mare Lane and follow this steeply up to **Pecorama Pleasure Gardens**, a local tourist attraction. At its entrance take a signposted public footpath ahead to reach its main car park, continuing along an obvious hedged track. Now out in open country, when you come to a T-junction go through a narrow hedge opening ahead and continue on the path across and then alongside fields.

You will see a permissive path signposted to nearby **Beer Quarry Caves**, a network of underground caverns created by the quarrying of local Beer stone. This creamy-white chalk limestone has been used in building work over many centuries; it is prized by masons because although it's quite soft and easy to cut when first mined, lending itself to fine detail carving, it dries and hardens when exposed to air and so is robust and lasts well. Beer stone has been used in famous buildings including St Paul's Cathedral, Westminster Abbey and the Tower of London, as well as many local churches and municipal buildings. There are tours of the caves, which incidentally are a very important site for various species of bat, including the Lesser and Greater Horseshoe varieties.

When a valley opens up ahead and Branscombe is glimpsed below, follow the path down the wooded hillside and go left before (not over) a stile and alongside a fence all the way down to join the road at the bottom. Here go right, along the road into the village and just before the junction (with

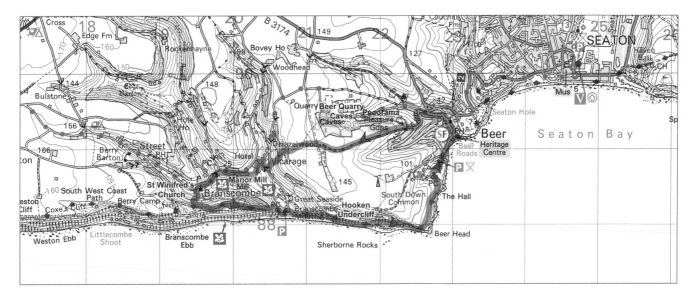

the Masons Arms ahead) turn left down a side road between houses. At the far end go over a footbridge and fork right on a path through the meadow. The path emerges by the National Trust's **Manor Mill**. *Dating from the 19th century, Manor Mill is a working water mill that once produced flour for local bread-making, as well as ground barley, oats and wheat for animal feed.*

Go ahead along the lane from the mill, then left on to the main thoroughfare through the (very strung-out) village of **Branscombe**. Pass the thatched Branscombe Forge and continue as far as **St Winifred's Church**.

Turn left and walk down through the churchyard for a public footpath that crosses a stream via a footbridge then climbs steeply up the wooded hillside to meet the coast path at the top. Turn left and follow this to the open viewpoint at the top of West Cliff. From here the shore is suddenly and very dramatically revealed far below. Go down the long, grassy slope all the way to **Branscombe Mouth**.

Of all the long-established regional trails included within the England Coast Path, there is surely none finer than the **South West Coast Path**, which is also covered by a separate Cicerone guidebook. In total, it stretches 1014km or 630 miles from Minehead in Somerset to Poole in Dorset and embraces the entire shorelines of Devon and Cornwall. As here at Branscombe and Beer, the route is efficiently signposted and waymarked, thanks in no small measure to the work of the South West Coast Path Association and its

▲ *Sea Shanty Beach Café at Branscombe Mouth*

volunteers. For over half a century this small charity has been helping to maintain and improve the route for walkers, it publishes an indispensable annual guidebook and is an all-round champion for coastal walking. To learn more about the organisation and to help with its work go to www. southwestcoastpath.org.uk.

Beyond the thatched beach café go over the bridge beside the ford, next to the car park, and turn right on to the coast path (signposted Beer). If you want to avoid an area of rougher ground below the cliffs ahead take the rising path to East Cliff and walk along the clifftop. Otherwise follow the waymarked route through a small linear caravan park squeezed below the cliffs. Beyond this the path weaves its way through a jumbled area known as **Hooken Undercliff**, until a stepped path takes you back up to the clifftop once more. *Hooken Undercliff came about in March 1790 following a huge cliff collapse, similar to the larger and better-known coastal slump between Axmouth and Lyme Regis just along to the east.*

Turn right and follow the broad, grassy clifftop via **Beer Head** back to the resort, swinging round via the edge of a

▲ *Looking west from Beer Head*

caravan park and car park before dropping down to the start of the walk along Common Lane and back into **Beer**.

There are several reasons to end your walk with a saunter on **the beach at Beer**. By the slipway, Beer Fisheries has a kiosk selling fresh catch, from plaice and monkfish to scallops and Dover sole. Just along from here is the excellent Fine Foundation Centre, a small visitor facility established by Beer Heritage Group to showcase Beer's coast and marine environment, with displays on everything from sealife and smuggling to the geology of the Jurassic Coast. There are handy cafés at the back of the shingle beach, where small fishing boats are hauled up by winch and holidaymakers enjoy their picnics. You also can't fail to notice the huge white cliffs that bookend the beach, since Beer is the furthest west that you will find chalk on the coast before the red sandstone and limestone take over.

Beach scavengers of today

Near the beach café at Branscombe is a very large anchor which once belonged to the MSC *Napoli*. When this South Africa-bound container ship ran aground at Branscombe Mouth on 18 January 2007, over 100 huge crates were lost overboard and their contents deposited on the shingle. And what an extraordinary array! From BMW motorbikes, shampoo, fertilisers and empty wine barrels to nappies, cat food, copies of the Bible and even family heirlooms. At first there were a few curious local onlookers, but then the media got hold of the story and crowds of modern-day scavengers headed for Branscombe from all over the country to see what they could find. Although many went away empty-handed, most of the motorbikes disappeared and many barrels found their way to a Somerset distillery, with most finders properly notifying the government's Receiver of Wreck who officially records cases of voluntary salvage wreck material. Local opinion remains divided whether it was simple opportunism or wanton vandalism. It took over two years and £50m to salvage and fully remove the *Napoli* and its cargo.

Walk 16

Lulworth

Start/Finish	Lulworth Cove (main car park) SY 821 800
Distance	13.75km (8.5 miles)
Total ascent	505m (1660ft)
Time	3hr 30min
Terrain	Broad downland tracks and clifftop paths, sometimes steep and may be slippery if wet
Map	OS OL15/OS Landranger 194
Refreshments	Various cafés, pubs and kiosks at Lulworth Cove and West Lulworth
Public transport	Daily buses from Weymouth serve Lulworth Cove from Easter to September
Parking	Lulworth Cove visitor car park (charge)

The rocks that have sculpted the dramatic shoreline of east Devon and Dorset, known as the Jurassic Coast, are big hitters. They have shaped our grandest buildings and assumed a profile way beyond simple mineral classification. On this walk you will gaze at the commanding lump of the Isle of Portland, famous for its durable building stone; while to the east is the equally prized limestone of Purbeck (see Walk 17). Sandwiched between them, here at Lulworth, is chalk, the coast's youngest rock (a mere 90 million years old). But perhaps more than the geology, it's the resultant coastal landforms that steal the show on this walk, including a much-photographed natural arch, dramatic folded rock strata and a rounded wave-cut bay enclosed by rocks that looks too perfectly formed to be true.

The walk starts at the far end of the main visitor car park at Lulworth Cove, where the popular route to Durdle Door begins. Go through the gate and leave the main track by turning immediately right for a waymarked path along the bottom of a slope through patchy scrub. Stay next to the fence and follow signs for the campsite above Durdle Door. The path swings left and goes up through open sloping fields. *Lulworth Cove was once served by two paddle steamers called the* Victoria *and* Empress *which brought thousands of holidaymakers from Weymouth, disembarking by ramps wheeled out into the water.*

After 1.2km you reach the caravan site and car park and here turn right for a wide track through a belt of trees next to the lane. Walk up to the bend at the top, cross over and follow the waymarked path through **Newlands Farm** following a sign for Ringstead.

This track soon opens out for a glorious, elevated and mostly level route across the top of the downs. The sea is over to the left and the Isle of Portland ahead. Maintain your direction almost due west across wide open pasture separated by occasional gates and fences, including a navigational beacon. At a set of gates on the very far side you can shorten the walk a little by veering left directly for White Nothe; otherwise go through the gate for a track indicated South Downs and Ringstead.

Now a magnificent panorama opens up inland, with a dry valley and large field barn immediately before you and the Wessex Downs filling the horizon. The wide and obvious bridleway ahead continues its no-nonsense direction through more fields, beginning to dip gently as it approaches Ringstead Bay.

Just past a large, thatched field barn, at a junction of tracks, go left on a surfaced track past the entrance to **Sea Barn Farm** and downhill. At roughly 7km from Lulworth this is the halfway point of the walk. There are fabulous views across Lyme Bay to Weymouth, Portland and the beginning of Chesil Beach.

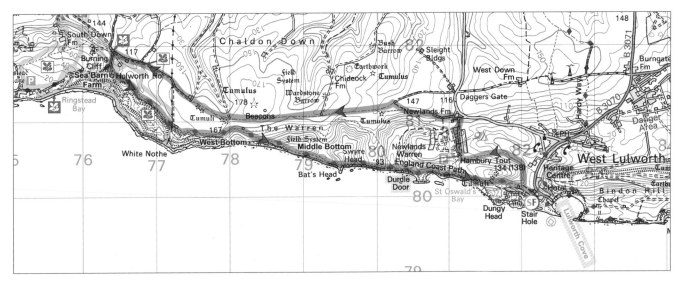

Looking west from the cliffs above Lulworth (photo: Chiz Dakin)

The **Isle of Portland** sits sphinx-like, a rigid lump of rock protruding off the end of the equally remarkable 13km shingle bank that is Chesil Beach. Pock-marked by huge quarries, active until quite recently and which have seen whole hillsides hewn out, as well as home to a prison and former naval base, Portland is not exactly a pretty place; but it has a rugged beauty and an individuality that extends beyond geology. Portlanders are (in the past, at least) an insular and superstitious bunch. One of their peculiarities is to never mention the name of a small, commonplace burrowing animal (the rabbit) for fear of bringing bad luck. Instead locals call apparently them 'underground mutton' and it's believed to originate from a time when quarry workers, seeing rabbits appearing from their burrows, believed they were responsible for perpetuating rockfalls and landslides.

At a junction of routes turn left at a signpost for the South West Coast Path. Follow this out across the top of the cliffs to

◀ *Cliff path east of White Nothe*

▲ *Durdle Door (photo: Chiz Dakin)* **119**

White Nothe, branching right at the former coastguard cottages to reach the clifftop viewpoint. *Near the prominent headland of White Nothe (literally 'white nose') is an area called Burning Cliff, which once caught fire because it's mainly made up of oil shale and iron pyrites.*

The return to Lulworth Cove (about 5.6km from this point) is along the well-walked and highly scenic clifftop path. There are fantastic views over the dramatic sequence of cliffs that stretch all the way to St Aldhelm's Head in the far distance, including **Middle Bottom** and **Bat's Head**, all offering stunning vantage points. Although route finding is no problem and the wide grassy strip back from the cliff edge allows plenty of space for you to choose your own route, some of the steep descents are rough in places and potentially slippery in wet weather.

The English coastline has many prominent memorials, towers and obelisks, often commemorating a noteworthy event or figure from history. However, on the clifftop above West Bottom are two slender **concrete pyramids**, about 6m high and placed at precise locations a short distance apart. These are not memorials or contemporary artwork but instead navigational sea marks which, when lined up, indicate to mariners the safe approach to Portland harbour from the south that avoids dangerous rock ledges and sand bank. A captain will take a compass bearing from the ship to the marks when the two appear in line and, together with others taken using different markers, buoys and beacons, plot intersecting lines that will inform the ship's course, speed and overall position.

Before long the spectacular limestone arch of **Durdle Door** appears ahead and no doubt you, like so many others, will feel the irresistible urge to take its photo. There are steps down to the beach opposite the arch. The equally picturesque bay to the east of the headland, framed by a line of rocks and cove known as The Man o'War, is also worth a detour.

Because of erosion the coast path has been diverted up the main visitor track from the caravan site and clifftop car park. At the brow of the hill, just before the car park, turn right on the track along the flank of Hambury Tout that descends to the car park at the start of the walk just west of **Lulworth Cove**.

The making of Lulworth Cove

The neat horseshoe bay of Lulworth Cove looks so perfectly shaped that it could have been fashioned by human hands. Think of a fan-like sea shell. In fact, it's a result of the sea penetrating the limestone barrier about 10,000 years ago, then eroding the softer clays behind, before meeting the more hard-wearing chalk that now forms the back of the bay. At the end of the walk also visit Stair Hole, just to the west of the cove, where the sea is slowly eroding the rock to form a new opening. Here can you also admire the splendidly named Lulworth Crumple, where the limestone strata has been twisted into dramatic folds. If that wasn't enough there's the remnants of a 145-million-year-old fossil forest to the east (when the army range path is open); and of course there are plenty of caves, blowholes and arches. To find out more about England's only natural World Heritage Site call in to the visitor centre at Lulworth Cove; and check out www.jurassiccoast.org.

Lulworth Cove

Seacombe Cliff (photo: Chiz Dakin)

Worth Matravers and St Aldhelm's Head

Start/Finish	Worth Matravers (car park) SY 974 776
Distance	12km (7.5 miles)
Total ascent	370m (1210ft)
Time	3hr
Terrain	Field and cliff paths, generally firm but a few steep slopes, including two long flights of steps
Map	OS OL15/OS Landranger 195
Refreshments	Square and Compass pub and Worth Matravers Tea & Supper Room
Public transport	Infrequent bus service from Swanage
Parking	Parish Council car park, Worth Matravers (charge)

This fine high-level walk around a prominent south coast headland would be a premier outing anywhere on the England Coast Path, but it's given added interest by what lies beneath your feet. Along the coast path are several small quarries, long since closed, that were chiselled and blasted out of the cliffs to access Purbeck's sought-after building stone. Much of the mining paraphernalia remains – galleries, ledges, a few old buildings – but of course the people are long gone, leaving behind a semi-industrial landscape that you can get up close to and touch. Here, from a remote coastal quarry in Dorset, came the raw materials that helped build and decorate some of the most prestigious public buildings in the land.

From the main visitor car park in Worth Matravers turn right and then go left at the junction by the Square and Compass pub. Head along the lane out of the village (whose name is locally shortened to Worth) and beyond the edge of the housing head diagonally right on a public footpath across fields to join a wide, walled bridleway, with the sea over to your right. *The bridleway is part of the Priest's Way, a 4.8km walking route from Swanage to Worth Matravers that traces the walking route of a local priest between his parishes.*

Continue in the same direction for 1.3km, past current and disused **quarries**, until a turning on the right with a stone marker indicating the footpath to Dancing Ledge. Follow this down towards the sea and, at a path junction beyond a gate on the left, head straight down towards the clifftop on a direct

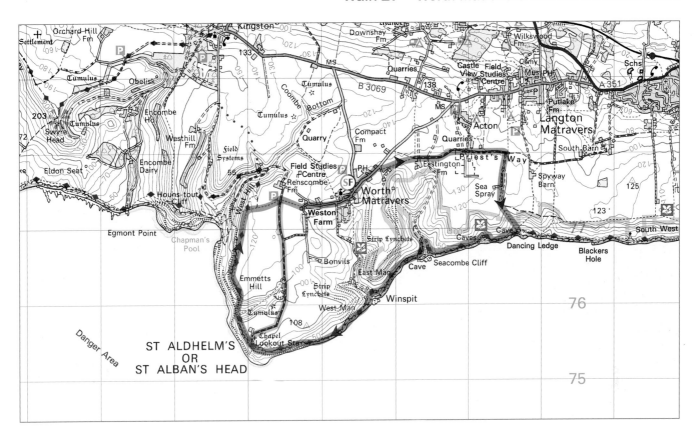

route across steeply sloping grass. The path joins the coast path at a stile giving access to **Dancing Ledge**.

Cross the stile for the stepped path down to the former quarry above the waves. There's plenty to see from the safety of the main stone platform, but to reach the broad lower ledge requires a little scrambling.

Dancing Ledge apparently gets its name from the fact that at high tides the waves wash over the lower ledge, or at least appear to dance as the seawater runs across the groves and hollows of the rock. However, another version describes how the rocky platform is roughly the size of a ballroom floor. On the left side of the ledge is a shallow, rectangular depression that was blasted out of the rock in the mid 20th century for use by local preparatory schools as a swimming pool. The schools may have gone but intrepid visitors still come here in their swimwear. It's not particularly large and you would only do a few strokes

before reaching the other end, but positioned just a few metres above the open sea, with the waves periodically spilling over into the pool, it does make for a unique wild swimming experience.

Return to the coast path and turn left. Follow the way-marked clifftop route along to **Seacombe Cliff**, where you have to kink inland to navigate the former quarry (you can divert to explore this too, if you wish). Go round a scrubby area of gorse and bramble and maintain your clifftop direction westwards. *At the site of these old quarries look out for organised groups climbing and abseiling on the vertical faces, as well as coasteering (clambering over the wave-splashed rocks and jumping into the sea).*

Continue on the clifftop path until you come to the remains of Winspit Quarry. Pause to look around this fascinating semi-industrial landscape; then follow the signs right and left around a thicket to climb back up to the clifftop once more. There are good views across Winspit Quarry and its caves and derelict structures from the elevated path.

The coast path sticks closely to the cliff edge, fortunately with a stout fence in between, and now makes for the prominent headland of **St Aldhelm's** (also called St Alban's), steepening significantly just before the point. At the top is a National Coastwatch Institution **lookout station** and nearby an historic **chapel**. *A simple but striking sculpture next to the path remembers the role that the location played in the development of radar during World War 2 (a nearby information panel has more details).*

Dedicated to St Aldhelm, the 7th-century Bishop of Sherborne who apparently sang his sermons in order to make them more appealing, this intriguing little **chapel** remains a place of worship and is open to visitors. Indeed, over the years its vaulted roof has offered shelter for coast path walkers keen to variously escape the sun, wind and rain. It was first mentioned in the 13th century, but little is known about its history or how it was used, other than as a useful navigation mark for passing sailors. A few interesting facts about the chapel, as well as some great tales about local legends and a mysterious grave discovered in a field nearby, are summarised in a booklet available in the chapel entrance.

The route now swings northwards and soon crosses a small but deep side valley – there are over 200 steps on both the steep down and up slopes! (If you want to avoid this section then follow the vehicle track inland from the chapel instead, which meets up with the route further on.) Go past a memorial to the Royal Marines on a high grassy path along the upper slope of **Emmetts Hill**. Ahead and far below is **Chapman's Pool**, surrounded by the slumped hillside below the towering cliffs of Houns-tout.

Look out for a turning on the right, signposted Renscombe, and from here follow a path across two fields to a small car park. Go out of the car park to cross the vehicle track from St Aldhelm's Head and take the field-edge path opposite to reach **Weston Farm**. Turn right on to the lane to walk through **Worth Matravers**, going left by the pub to return to the start of the walk.

One of only a handful of pubs to have been listed in every single edition of CAMRA's Good Beer Guide, the **Square and Compass** is a fine village inn that has retained its character and continued to be lively and welcoming, without turning into a pastiche or museum piece. Named very fittingly (given the location) after tools used by stonemasons, the pub has its own rock and fossil collection housed in a small museum on the premises. The Square and Compass hosts regular music and beer festivals, including themes such as beer and pumpkin, and cider and sausage. Inside there are original flagstone floors and simple wooden benches, but no bars, as such. Instead, drinks are served through a traditional hatch from rows of barrels lined up on what's known as a stillage. It's a rare sight these days.

The legacy of Purbeck's coastal quarries

For centuries the limestone of Purbeck has been prized as a building material, with Portland stone and Purbeck marble (fossilised limestone) featuring in many notable British buildings, including Westminster Abbey and Canterbury Cathedral. Since the rock strata occurs naturally at various coastal locations, quarries like Dancing Ledge, Seacombe and Winspit sprang up and produced vast quantities of stone. It was lowered straight into waiting boats before being shipped off to (literally) pave the streets of London. The ledges and caves were carved out of the cliff-face just above the waves and the larger caves or galleries even have crude rock pillars supporting the roofs. They are incredibly atmospheric and evocative places, so much so that Winspit doubled up as both the planet Mercon II in the 1970s TV series *Blake's 7* (where it was a mine for Feldon crystal) and the planet Skaro from *Destiny of the Daleks* in a *Doctor Who* serial from 1979. As recently as May 2021 it was also used as a filming location for the *Star Wars* television series *Andor*.

▲ *Dancing Ledge (photo: Chiz Dakin)*

South East

The Solent to The Wash

The south east is inevitably the most developed part of the English coast, with large population centres, industry and transport hubs; but if you think it's an endless urban trudge all the way from The Solent to The Wash you couldn't be more wrong. This is a varied and historic coast where built-up areas are punctuated by bursts of natural beauty. It's generally easy walking, made highly accessible thanks to good public transport links.

Nowhere is this juxtaposition more obvious than at Chichester Harbour (Walk 18), where you can explore the extensive and peaceful network of tidal channels just a short distance from Portsmouth and Southampton. Heading east, between

High and dry on the shingle at Dungeness (photo: Chiz Dakin, Walk 20)   127

the hubbub of Brighton and the gentility of Eastbourne is a superb, high-level walk along the undulating chalk cliffs of the Seven Sisters (Walk 19) in the South Downs National Park.

As elsewhere around England, the south east is full of remarkable contrasts when it comes to coastal habitats. Dungeness (Walk 20) has one of the largest areas of vegetated shingle in Europe, and a circular route around this surprisingly remote and unusual landscape reveals a unique natural and human history.

The Kent shoreline is synonymous with defence and invasion, as well as our sometimes uneasy relationship with continental Europe, and Martello Towers and castles are visible reminders of a confrontational past. Walk 21 along the White Cliffs of Dover captures the history and symbolism of this famous coastline – and is a superb walking route, too.

North of the Thames Estuary the low-lying coastlines of Essex and Suffolk are riddled with creeks and marshes, where sinuous estuaries reach deep into the land. It's atmospheric rather than dramatic, with gentle walking that uncovers a wealth of local stories, such as at Tollesbury (Walk 22) by the mouth of the River Blackwater. It's an easy outing, too, at Orford in Suffolk (Walk 23), but here attention turns to the enigmatic shingle spit across the water with a top secret past.

East Anglia's low and open coast makes it vulnerable to major weather events, such as at Dunwich, near Southwold. Walk 24 crosses marsh, coastal heath and shoreline in search of a once-thriving town that succumbed to the sea many centuries ago. To the north there are equally big skies and wide horizons in Norfolk, where a weekend route along the salt-marshes, sand and shingle shore between Burnham Deepdale and Sheringham (Walk 25) on the north coast visits a string of outstanding nature reserves – so remember to take your binoculars.

▲ *Creeks and marshes off Tollesbury (photo: Chiz Dakin, Walk 22)* ▶ *Bosham from across the water (photo: Shirley Rushmer)*

Walk 18

Bosham and Chichester Harbour

Start/Finish	Bosham Quay SU 803 037
Distance	16.5km (10.2 miles)
Total ascent	10m (30ft)
Time	5hr
Terrain	Flat fields and woodland paths, shingle foreshore, may be wet underfoot in places, and some paths are tidal - see below
Map	OS OL8/OS Landranger 197
Refreshments	Shoreside Café at Bosham, Quarterdeck Café at Itchenor and Boat House Café at Chichester Marina, plus several pubs
Public transport	Bus service to Bosham from Chichester, Mon to Sat
Parking	Main car park at Bosham (charge)
Note	This walk requires the use of a foot ferry to Itchenor (runs daily, March to September, weekends only the rest of the year) and two short sections of the route may be impassable at high tide – for local tide times go to www.conservancy.co.uk
Warning	Bosham open shore-side road floods every high tide, so be sure to use the main car park instead

Chichester Harbour is a huge tidal estuary with a resident fleet of 12,000 boats, 3500 moorings and 14 separate sailing clubs. Its smooth blue tentacles penetrate deep into the leafy countryside of Hampshire and West Sussex, with yachts and motor vessels of all description moored up in marinas and private berths. For the most part the coast path stays close to the tranquil shoreline of woodland, fields and some well-heeled villages; but it's also an important place for wildlife, particularly birds, and one of the few places on England's south coast that remains relatively undeveloped. This easy and engrossing waterside walk is based on one of a series of excellent local routes promoted by Chichester Harbour Conservancy, see www.conservancy.co.uk.

From the quayside at Bosham (pronounced "Bozz-um"), beside the Quay Master's office, walk eastwards along the open shoreline road around the edge of the channel or estuary arm, taking a short cut across the exposed bed on a low tide causeway if it's safe to do so. At high tide follow the pathway above the road, which on the far side is a footpath along the field edge. Near a large house called The Saltings leave the lane for a sign-posted public footpath around the foreshore of the peninsula. If high tide prevents access to this section simply stay on the lane until the bend near **Ferry Barn**, then walk down to the shore.

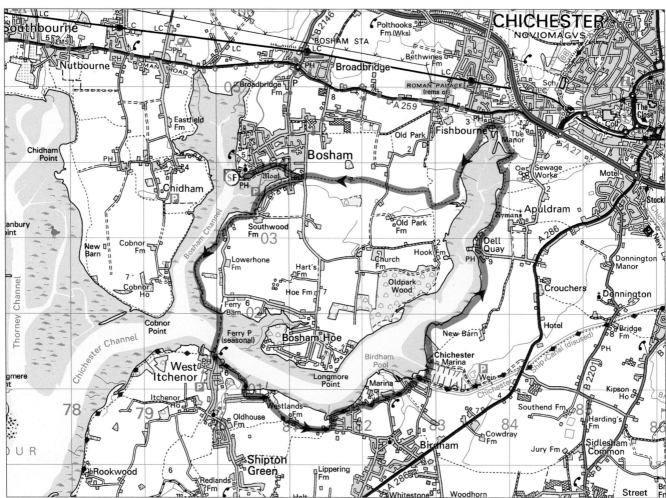

After 1.6km Itchenor draws level across the wide channel and there is a sign for the foot ferry. A short path leads across the marsh and mudflats to the water's edge and there are three separate landing stages depending on the state of the tide. *Although the map still refers to West Itchenor, most people know it simply as Itchenor, as East Itchenor seems to have simply been a manor house that disappeared centuries ago.*

There has been a **passenger ferry** at Itchenor since the 17th century, saving a very long walk around Chichester Channel via Fishbourne. Although it ceased for a few years, the service was brought back by Chichester Harbour Conservancy in 1976 in order to join up the footpath network and provide a water taxi for moored boats. It operates all year round (weekends only between September and March) and is moored at the jetty at Itchenor. To summon it from the opposite bank simply walk down to the landing point and give a big wave. Although the ride takes barely five minutes the view of the harbour from the water is rewarding – and it's great fun! To check times and availability go to www.itchenorferry.co.uk.

Once back on dry land, from Itchenor jetty walk up the road into the village and turn left opposite the Ship Inn to regain the shore. Turn right by the sailing club and follow the path until it veers inland between large houses. Turn left along a private drive and at the end go right on a path through woods and across fields. Join a metalled lane past **Westlands Farm** and turn left and left again following public footpath signs to get back to the shore. The path then heads inland once more and at a junction of lanes go left to reach **Birdham Pool Marina**.

Walk past the boatyard, with its impressive crane that can lift vessels weighing 30 tonnes, and at the road bend go straight on along the path to cross the canal gate at Salterns Lock. Go past the yacht club and into **Chichester Marina**. *Chichester Marina is one of the UK's largest with over 1000 berths, a hive of nautical activity with extensive boatyards, chandlers and marine services of all description.*

Turn left in front of the main buildings and café. Cross the entrance to the marina via the lock gate (you may have to wait if several vessels are passing through). Entering woodland on the far side, take the left fork and emerging into fields follow a

▲ *Bosham and Chichester Harbour (Photo: Brian Bacher/Compass Photography Services)*

long-established and popular permissive path out beside the edge of Fishbourne Channel, until after 2.4km you reach **Dell Quay**.

Like many of the villages dotted around Chichester Harbour, **Dell Quay** has a small boatyard, sailing club and a long association with the sea. Two thousand years ago Roman galleys sailed all the way up past Itchenor and Dell Quay to Fishbourne, where it's thought they had a military base (and which is today best known for its well-preserved Roman Palace). In the Middle Ages, Dell Quay was a main landing point for cargoes in and out of Chichester, with wool and grain being exported and the likes of coal and wine coming in. Boat-building at Itchenor also goes back several centuries, carried on today by Haines' Boatyard. When this historic local business was put up for sale in the 1980s it was purchased by a group of yachtsmen from Itchenor Sailing Club who now run the thriving company.

At the Crown & Anchor pub by the waterside turn right and beyond a small boatyard follow a succession of easy paths along the edge of the channel until you get to its head at Fishbourne Meadows on the edge of **Fishbourne**. Don't go any further into the village, but instead turn left and walk beside a shady stream, then out across a reed bed on a firm path that is prone to flooding for a short while at high tide.

Now walk back along the peaceful far shoreline with views across the water to the distant spire of Chichester Cathedral. The path eventually swings west, across a field, and at the far side go right then left. Follow a series of field paths almost due west. Cross two roads and re-enter **Bosham** via a passageway between houses, with the quay ahead. *Despite the warning signs, some first-time visitors leave their cars on Bosham's open shore-side road, returning to see them swamped by the tide – locals call it the 'Bosham car wash'.*

Balancing recreation and conservation

As with so many protected and environmentally sensitive areas that are also popular and accessible, a careful balance has to be struck between conservation and recreation. At Chichester Harbour the human activity is as much on water as on land, with everything from paddle boarders and dinghies to yachts and motor cruisers. But, of course, this is also the destination for 55,000 waders and wildfowl on their annual migration. Despite this, the shape and size of the harbour is large enough to absorb its many users and offer some rewarding wildlife moments. Indeed, it's remarkable how quiet and rural this location, an area of outstanding natural beauty, can feel, even though Portsmouth is just down the road. If you have time for another coastal walk here, a wonderful shoreline path stretches from Itchenor out to East Head, a tidal spit of sand dune and shingle at the mouth of Chichester Harbour by West Wittering (there-and-back about 11.3km).

◄ *Boats leaving Chichester Marina*　　　　▲ *Motorists are regularly caught out by Bosham's tidal road*　　**133**

Walk 19
Seaford to Eastbourne

Start	Seaford (eastern end of Esplanade) TV 484 985
Finish	Eastbourne (pier) TV 617 989
Distance	21km (13 miles)
Total ascent	640m (2100ft)
Time	5hr 30min
Terrain	Wide and undulating grassy clifftop with a few steep slopes, plus riverbank and promenade
Map	OS Explorer OL25/OS Landranger 199
Refreshments	Lots of choice in Seaford and Eastbourne, cafés at visitor centres at Seven Sisters Country Park (near Exceat Bridge) and Birling Gap
Public transport	Both Seaford and Eastbourne have train stations and an hourly bus service runs between Seaford and Eastbourne via Exceat Bridge every day
Parking	Seaford Esplanade car park and Eastbourne (charge)

Seven Sisters from Cuckmere Haven (photo: Fiona Barltrop)

There's a certain elemental and rhythmic pleasure in traversing a line of gently undulating chalk cliffs on foot. The Seven Sisters, a flowing white curtain on England's south coast, offers a combination of relatively easy and uncomplicated walking with springy turf underfoot, plus a sense of constant elevation and supreme sea views. There's always a temptation to jog on the downward slopes, but perhaps instead try counting the sisters in turn, as there's arguably a half one (although calling them the Seven and a Half Sisters doesn't have the same ring to it). With handily placed refreshment points and an excellent daily bus service allowing for a linear outing, this is an accessible south coast walking adventure that can be enjoyed by all ages.

The walk starts at the eastern end of Seaford Esplanade by **Martello Tower** No 74, which is now Seaford's Local History Museum.

Martello Towers resemble giant stone sandcastles and feature at the beginning and end of this walk. They were built around the south east coast of England during the early 1800s to provide defence in the face of a threat of invasion by Napoleon. Named after an original version on

Mortella Point on Corsica, these squat little fortresses were built with thick walls designed to withstand attack and were in effect mini garrisons containing living and sleeping quarters for soldiers, with cannon positioned on the roof. The French never did invade, of course, so the Martello Towers remained untested. Today some are museums or can be visited, like at Seaford and Eastbourne, others are used for accommodation and the rest are now derelict.

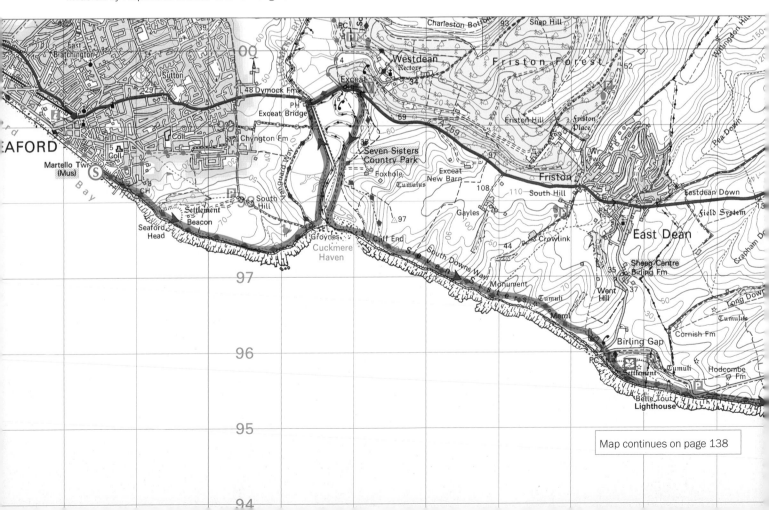

Map continues on page 138

View along the Seven Sisters towards Birling Gap (photo: Fiona Barltrop)

Follow the steep but popular path up to the top of **Seaford Head**, alongside the golf course. As with the rest of the walk, the path is in fact a very broad grassy strip that extends back from the cliff edge and is bordered by fields and scrub. Soon there are excellent views back along the Sussex coast to Newhaven and distant Brighton. *Along the walk you may see waymarks for two long distance walking trails that connect Greater London with the south coast: the Vanguard Way (Croydon to Newhaven) and Wealdway (Gravesend to Eastbourne).*

Descend to the former coastguard cottages above Cuckmere Haven, where there is a classic and much-photographed view looking eastwards along the entire Seven Sisters. Walk down past the cottages to the shingle beach of **Cuckmere Haven** and turn left to follow the bank of the river upstream, and 5km after leaving Seaford arrive at **Exceat Bridge** by the Cuckmere Inn. *The sign outside the pub bears the Latin inscription* E Ventis vires *which is Seaford's Coat of Arms and means 'strength from the wind'.*

You will notice that your route inland to Exceat Bridge is along a very straight section of the river, while on the way back out you will be close to the original meanders. '**The**

Cut' was created in 1847 in an attempt to make the river navigable for trade and also to alleviate flooding, since the Cuckmere often flooded as far up as the historic settlement of Alfriston. In recent years there have been suggestions from environmentalists, opposed by local landowners, that the artificial levees of the cut should no longer be repaired when they breach and the lower Cuckmere allowed to flood naturally once more. It's another example of the dilemma thrown up by climate change and rising sea levels, and at what point (or whether) natural processes should be allowed to take over once more.

On the far side of Exceat Bridge turn right and walk the pavement to reach Seven Sisters Country Park **visitor centre** (toilets and café) and from here a well-walked track leads back down the valley to Cuckmere Haven.

Now on the eastern side of the river's mouth, a sign states that it takes three hours to walk from here to Birling Gap along the beach below the cliffs, but only on a falling tide. However, a safer, scenic and more enjoyable route is to clamber up the steep slope of Cliff End for the exhilarating **Seven Sisters** rollercoaster.

Although the cliff edge is unfenced, the close-cropped turf strip is extremely wide and there is plenty of room to spread out and safely enjoy the constantly undulating route over (in turn) Haven Brow, Short Brow, Rough Brow, Brass Point, Flat Hill, Baily's Hill and Went Hill.

A fenced track eventually leads down off Went Hill past buildings to **Birling Gap**, where there is a National Trust visitor centre and café on top of the cliffs. A staircase gives access to the beach.

The clifftop route continues up the gently sloping slope. Go past the former **Belle Tout lighthouse**, while on the shore far below is its famous red and white striped replacement. *The newer lighthouse was opened in 1902 at the foot of Beachy Head's towering cliffs, after problems with erosion and sea mist rendered Belle Tout unviable and ineffective.*

Climb steadily to the top of **Beachy Head**, at 162m the high-point on the route with panoramic views over the English Channel.

To reach Eastbourne, about 5km away, keep the clifftop pub and countryside centre over to your left and follow a way-marked public footpath on the right down to reach the RAF memorial on the edge of the cliffs. At a junction of routes go right, down a long steep grassy slope, for an obvious and well-used path that shadows the cliff edge and swings round towards the town. This continues above a thicket, past some football pitches and via a semi-surfaced track emerges at a popular café called The Kiosk. Here you will find a smart South Downs Way sign marking the start of the National Trail on its 161km journey to Winchester.

Turn right and walk down the pavement towards the town centre. After Helen Garden branch right down Holywell Drive to access the promenade, which will lead you all the way to the finish by **Eastbourne** pier. Just before this is the Wish Tower, otherwise known as Martello Tower No 73.

The movable lighthouse

There are signs aplenty warning visitors to stay back from the unfenced cliff edge because of rock falls, not least because researchers say that the chalk is eroding at between 22–32cm a year. This has posed a particular problem for Belle Tout lighthouse above Birling Gap. When it was built in 1834 the Grade II listed building was situated comfortably back from the cliff edge, but 185 years and many rock falls later it found itself just four precarious metres from the drop. So, in an impressive feat of civil engineering, 22 hydraulic jacks were used to lift the entire 850-ton structure on to four steel-topped concrete beams and move it (very slowly) 17 metres back from the cliff edge. All is well for now, at least, but cliff erosion is unpredictable and accelerating, especially in the face of more extreme weather conditions, so one estimate is that Belle Tout may well end up on the cliff edge again in as little as 25 years.

▲ *Belle Tout lighthouse from Beachy Head*

Walk 20

Dungeness

Start/Finish	Dungeness (old lighthouse) TR 088 169
Distance	14km (8.7 miles)
Total ascent	10m (30ft)
Time	3hr 30min
Terrain	Flat vegetated shingle and open shingle beach, road
Map	OS Explorer 125/OS Landranger 189
Refreshments	Britannia Inn and The Pilot pub at Dungeness, End of the Line café at Dungeness Station (open every day the trains are running and over winter weekends) and Dungeness Fish Hut
Public transport	Daily buses from Ashford and Dover (as far as The Pilot pub)
Parking	Car park near Dungeness Station
Note	Dogs on lead on section through RSPB reserve

Dungeness is different to almost anywhere else on the English coast. Quite apart from the fact that it is one of the largest areas of vegetated shingle in Europe, nationally important for its plants, insects and birds, this bare and tree-less landscape stuck out on the far side of Romney Marsh has a palpable remoteness, but also an edgy frontier spirit. Wooden cabins and artists' shacks are randomly scattered across the boundary-less shingle; a narrow-gauge steam railway just seems to end in the middle of nowhere; two separate lighthouses stare silently out to sea; and all the while a hulking nuclear power station thrums away incongruously in the background. For the curious coastal walker (and you will be curious, believe me) this is an other-worldly outpost of amazing light, atmosphere and baffling juxtaposition that challenges conventional notions of coastal beauty.

The walk starts at the public car park near the railway terminus. Facing the old (black-painted) lighthouse turn right towards the power station. Turn left before the station's perimeter wall and follow the driveway towards the sea. Walk over the shingle bank and down to the water's edge, then turn right and follow the foreshore for 2.3km. This is the route of the England Coast Path and a public right of way. It can be slow-going underfoot, but at least the high shingle bank mostly keeps

Dungeness power station out of sight. *There are two nuclear power stations here. Dungeness A, nearest the lighthouses, and Dungeness B which, when it became operational in 1983, was the UK's first advanced gas-cooled reactor. Both are now being decommissioned.*

At the far end, where the bank levels out, continue along the shoreline until you reach a vehicle track by a lookout post. Turn right and follow this bumpy, unmade lane beside a

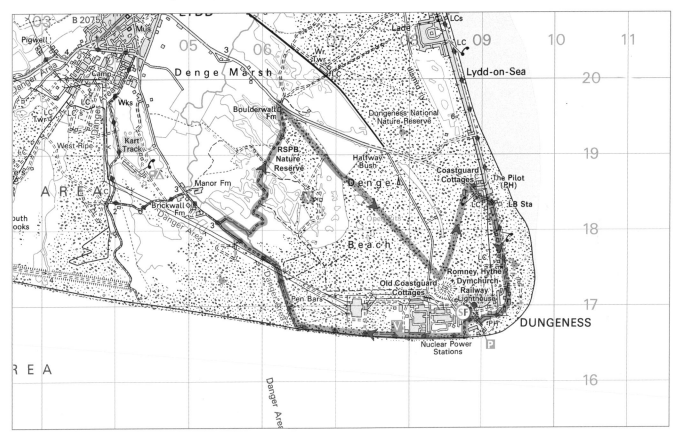

Reedy lakes at RSPB Dungeness (photo: Chiz Dakin)

fenced-off military firing range. After 1.6km take a waymarked bridleway on the right that first crosses a stone bridge then swings right, beside a broad, water-filled channel. The track then turns left and takes a winding route all the way across the RSPB's Dungeness **Nature Reserve**. There are connecting paths to the nearby visitor centre.

The **nature reserve** is based on a series of flooded gravel pits, interspersed with shingle, low undergrowth, fen and meadows. Star species include bittern, which breed here, plus marsh harrier, bearded tit, lapwing and Little ringed plover. In summer, terns and gulls nest on the beach, while winter ducks such as smew and Slavonian grebe are regular sights. Jutting out into the sea at one of the narrowest parts of the English Channel, Dungeness is an excellent location to see passing migrants, from wheatears and warblers to swallows and ospreys. There are two waymarked walking trails and various hides dotted across the reserve. Binocular hire is available from the visitor centre, which also keeps a list of all the latest sightings.

At a junction where the bridleway meets the main vehicle route to the visitor centre go straight ahead, along the gravel drive, until just before the gateway at the far end by **Boulderwall Farm**. Don't go out on the main road but turn sharply right, by a public footpath signpost. The faint path crosses an area of shingle and patchy grass. Keep close to a lake visible through bushes on the left.

Continue ahead on a narrow strip of land between two lakes and then go across the bare shingle of **Denge Beach**. The route is intermittently indicated by low wooden posts with faded yellow arrows, but make sure to aim for the old **lighthouse** to the left of the power station ahead and you won't go far wrong.

The route finally reaches the road to the power station, which it crosses via gates in the fence. On the far side continue in the same direction along a thin path until you get to a high, circular grassy bank that encloses the **Old Coastguard Cottages**.

Turn sharply left, away from the cottages, through a line of wooden posts and on along a straight, clear path through

▲   *Prospect Cottage was once the home of film director Derek Jarman*

patchy undergrowth and then across open shingle for just under 1.6km to reach **Coastguard Cottages**. Pass to the right of the buildings and at a junction turn right through the white-gated entrance into the Dungeness Estate. Follow this unfenced road out towards the tip of the ness.

There are marked paths and a boardwalk across the shingle from the road to the water's edge, if you want to go right down to the sea at this point. General public access to the wider foreshore is restricted to protect the many **unusual and fragile plants** that have made their home in this national nature reserve, including yellow horned poppy, wild carrot and sea kale. Quite remarkably, given the inhospitable habitat of shingle and salt-laden winds, Dungeness is home to 600 species of plants, which is a third of all plants found in the UK. In addition, other notable **wildlife** found here include the pygmy footman moth, great crested newt and medicinal leech. This is the largest British leech and the only one able to suck blood from humans.

Go over the level crossing and on past the **lifeboat station**. On your right is a seemingly random string of odd one-storey cottages, some little more than large sheds and cabins, and many converted from railway wagons and carriages that were once dragged across the shingle. A few are now artists' studios and from another local fishermen sell their fresh catch, which is also served up as tasty snacks at the next-door Dungeness Fish Hut. Prospect Cottage was once home to the renowned film director Derek Jarman whose creative and naturalistic garden still draws visitors to this day. Running behind the cottages is the 15-inch gauge Romney, Hythe & Dymchurch Railway. *Kent's so-called 'mainline in miniature' runs 22km and has been transporting visitors on its one-third full size steam and diesel locomotives for almost a century, see* www.rhdr.org.uk.

At a fork keep straight on past the new lighthouse which, rather unusually, is floodlit at night to help vessels identify it but also to prevent bird mortality during the migration season. Continue via the Britannia Inn and finish by the **old lighthouse** and the railway terminus.

Britain's only desert

An incredibly barren landscape sometimes described as Britain's only desert, Dungeness is what's known as a cuspate foreland (or ness), a highly distinctive coastal feature created over time by longshore drift. Waves approach the coastline from an angle and push sand, sediment and shingle on to and along the shore through their constant action. This movement can be in any direction, but where material is pushed from two different directions at once it can result in ridges that combine to form a triangular extension of the coastline, such as here at Dungeness where the angle between the two main shorelines is particularly acute. A cuspate foreland can measure anything from a few metres to several kilometres and although larger ones can become well established, even held together by vegetation like here, it's a landform that often continues to evolve and move position because of the relentless power of the sea. Other notable cuspate forelands include Cape Kennedy in Florida, Point Pelee on Lake Erie in Ontario, Canada, and Cabo Santa Maria on the Portuguese Algarve.

Dungeness is one of the largest areas of vegetated shingle in Europe (photo: Chiz Dakin)

Walk 21
Deal to Dover

Start	Deal (pier) TR 378 526
Finish	Dover (Marine Parade) TR 320 411
Distance	15.5km (9.6 miles)
Total ascent	500m (1640ft)
Time	4hr
Terrain	Flat promenade and high chalk cliffs, a few fairly modest slopes
Map	OS Explorer 138/OS Landranger 179
Refreshments	Pubs, cafés and shops in Deal, Walmer, Kingsdown, St Margaret's at Cliffe and Dover
Public transport	Regular daily trains between Deal and Dover
Parking	Town centre in Deal or Dover (charge)

Few landmarks on the England Coast Path are so iconic and have such cultural significance than the White Cliffs of Dover. For some, they may be a symbol of home or evoke a notion of sovereignty; but with France in sight on a clear day, little more than 32km across the Channel, they are also our tangible interface with mainland Europe. This relatively easy walk along the lofty chalk cliffs that form Kent's south eastern seaboard remind us of our continental bonds, from Julius Caesar's arrival in 55BC to the incessant cross-Channel ferry traffic today; or, the regular text alerts that you may well receive, with phone providers mistakenly thinking you're in France!

Facing the sea by the pier in Deal turn right and walk along the promenade. Pass the Time Ball Tower museum, **castle** and bandstand and continue amid the dog-walkers, joggers and cyclists to **Walmer**, at which point the popular thoroughfare gets a little less busy. Make sure to stay out of the well-used but clearly segregated cycle lane.

The Time Ball Tower at Deal – the ball drops down the mast every hour to tell passing ships the time

Deal is one of a string of attractive old towns that line the coast of south east England. Some are historic Cinque Ports, established in the Middle Ages to provide the Crown with men and ships before a standing navy was established. Although Deal was associated with this network, many of its residents preferred the rather less lawful pursuit of smuggling, for which they were renowned. The town's seafaring association persists today with sailing and rowing regattas, sea angling competitions and an annual maritime and folk festival. In particular, pause to admire the Time Ball Tower, with its short mast at the top down which a ball drops every hour to send an accurate Greenwich Mean Time signal to passing ships.

The flat route continues along the back of the shingle beach past a long line of bungalows, chalets and holiday homes to reach the Zetland Arms at **Kingsdown**. The pub takes its name from a ship called the *Earl of Zetland* that was wrecked on this coast in 1860.

Continue across a small patch of open shingle at the back of the beach and where the coast road bends sharply inland. Go up steps on to the cliffs, which is the first climb of the day. The route soon levels out for a broad and grassy clifftop strip and 3.4km after leaving Kingsdown you arrive at the towering war memorial near **Bockhill Farm**. *The tall stone pillar commemorates the sacrifice of almost 2000 men of the*

◀ *Looking towards Dover from above Langdon Bay (photo: Chiz Dakin)*

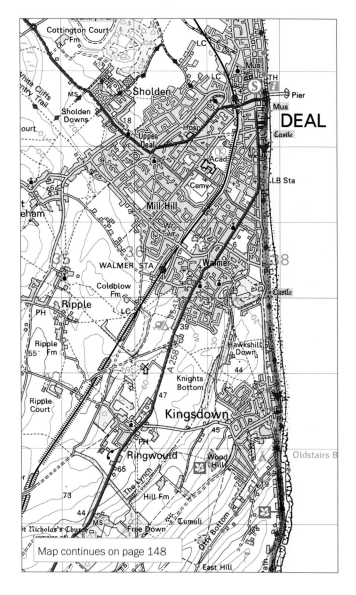

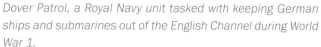

Map continues on page 148

Dover Patrol, a Royal Navy unit tasked with keeping German ships and submarines out of the English Channel during World War 1.

The elevated path offers good views of the imposing chalk cliffs ahead and soon begins to drop down to **St Margaret's at Cliffe**. Follow the path past houses, then look out for coast path waymarks that send you down a series of steep steps to the beach car park below. Turn right past the café and toilets.

From the shore head up the road next to the Coastguard pub, then left along Beach Road past **The Pines Garden** tea room and museum. Turn left at the signpost for a short path back out to the open clifftop once more. Join a wide track landwards of some private properties until, after 1.6km, you reach **South Foreland lighthouse**.

With its short, squat appearance and castellated finish, **South Foreland lighthouse** has a defensive feel about it,

▲ *South Foreland lighthouse (photo: Chiz Dakin)*

which seems appropriate given its location on the top of the White Cliffs. There have been beacons here since Roman times, in particular to warn ships of the nearby Goodwin Sands. This notorious 16km sand bank has accounted for hundreds of vessels over the centuries, many literally sucked into the shifting sand and never seen again. The present lighthouse dates from Victorian times and was the first in the world to use a light powered by electricity. It's now owned by the National Trust and is open daily in season, plus there's a handy tearoom that passing walkers can also enjoy.

The final 3.2km of the clifftop walking route is a superb, unbroken section along the undulating chalk cliffs that is as easy and obvious to follow as it is popular. Indeed, given the location's high profile, accessibility and nearness to the ferry port, you will likely hear a range of tongues from many different countries. *Along this section you pass the entrance to Fan*

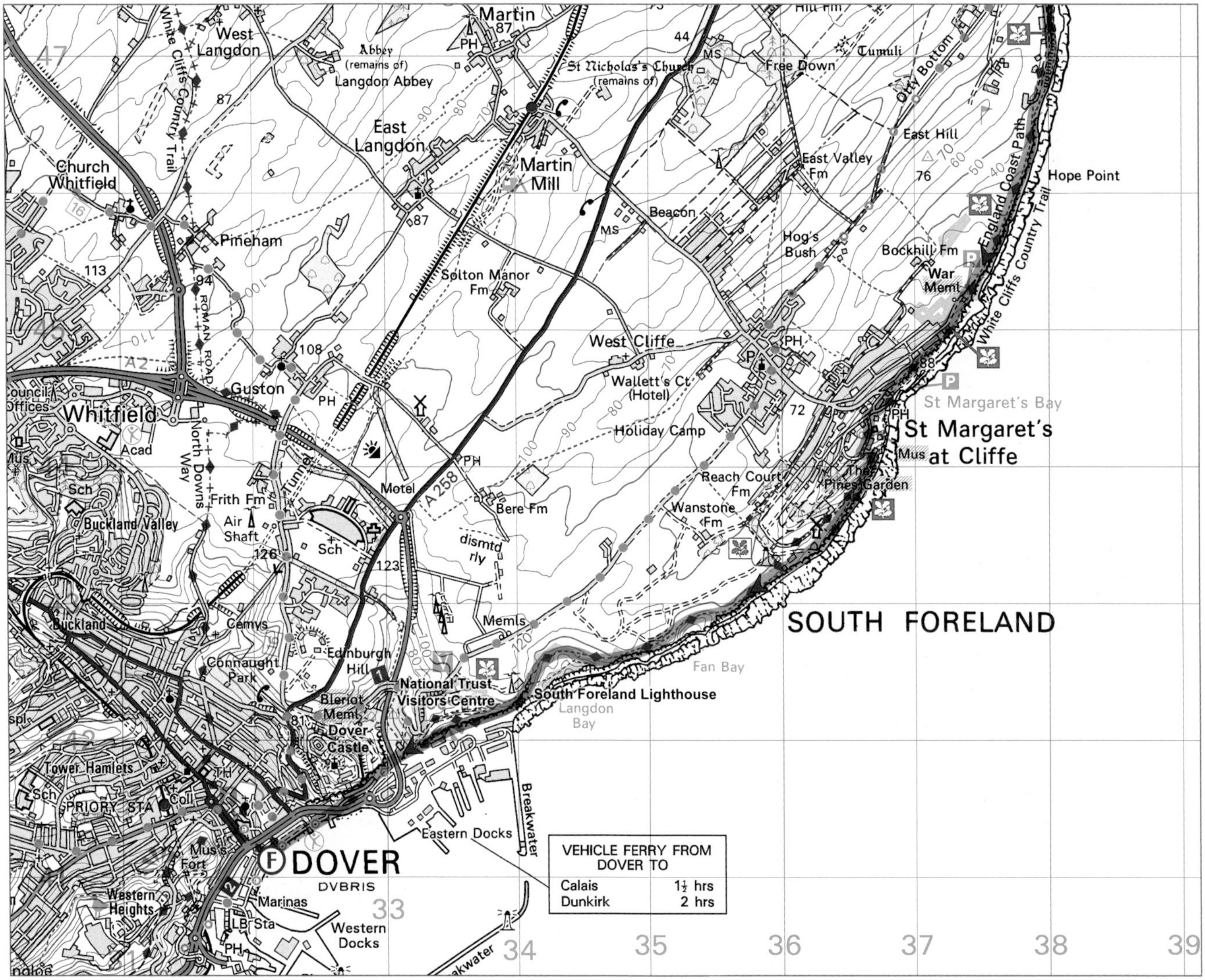

Bay Deep Shelter, a tunnel complex dug between 1940 and 1941 for the gun emplacement above, and open periodically for guided visits.

The route passes **Langdon Bay** and the National Trust visitor centre and café, although all eyes are drawn seawards towards the never-ending procession of cross-Channel ferries entering and leaving Dover's Eastern Docks just a short distance below the cliffs. The harbour-side is a place of constant activity, with the occasional tannoy announcements sometimes drifting up from below.

Beyond the visitor centre and car park go out to the road. At the hairpin bend, with **Dover Castle** on the hilltop ahead, go straight on and down a steep, surfaced path underneath a flyover to enter the town. Walk ahead along a narrow street called East Cliff, then cross the main road via pedestrian lights to turn right and along the edge of the harbour. The walk finishes in **Dover** by the public sculpture celebrating cross-Channel swimming, called *On the Crest of a Wave*, next to the start of the North Downs Way National Trail.

▶ *Dover's Eastern Docks at twilight (photo: Chiz Dakin)*

'Nothing great is easy' reads the inscription on the memorial to Matthew Webb in his home town of Dawley in Shropshire; and as the first person to **swim across the English Channel** in 1875 he certainly proved the point. Captain Webb took 21 hours to complete the feat, but now the record for this highly demanding long-distance open water swim is down to 6 hours 55 minutes. According to the Channel Swimming Association (CSA), the changing currents and unpredictable weather conditions mean that you actually swim much further than you envisage, through one of the busiest shipping lanes in the world in very cold water that's full of jellyfish! The CSA website has plenty of handy tips for aspiring swimmers, including whether you need to take a passport or smear grease over your body, and whether there are sharks in the Channel (answer: 'It is too cold for most sharks... and sightings are so rare that you won't need a cage!').

Tunnels, castles and clifftop defences

When the Channel Tunnel opened in 1994 it finally provided a solid link between Britain and continental Europe that had first been suggested almost two centuries before. The tunnel heads out just to the west of Dover and spoil from the massive construction project created a new country park at the foot of the cliffs called Samphire Hoe. However, the stern outline of Dover Castle which overlooks the town is testament to a more troubled relationship with our neighbours. The 12th-century fortress is one of the largest in England and soldiers gazing out across the water towards Cap Gris-Nez would have been well aware of their vulnerability to attack, which continued even into modern times, when Dover was the first place in Britain to suffer a bombing raid from the air (and later earned the nickname 'Hellfire Corner'). The castle retains its extensive tunnel system, which during World War 2 made it an important military command centre, including a central role in the evacuation of Dunkirk.

▲ *Dover Castle (photo: Chiz Dakin)* ▶ *Tollesbury's peaceful moorings (photo: Chiz Dakin)*

Tollesbury and the Blackwater Estuary

Start/Finish	Tollesbury (Woodrolfe Road car park) TL 963 106
Distance	15km (9.3 miles)
Total ascent	70m (230ft)
Time	3hr 30min
Terrain	Grassy sea wall, paths, pavements and country lanes
Map	OS Explorer 176/OS Landranger 168
Refreshments	The Loft tea room and Harbour View bistro and bar, both at Tollesbury Marina
Public transport	Buses to Tollesbury from Maldon and Colchester (Mon to Sat)
Parking	Woodrolfe Road car park, Tollesbury
Note	Dogs on lead through nature reserves

Because of its many indentations, estuaries and islands, the overall length of the Essex coast (905km) is second only to Cornwall's (1086km). And although it may not have any soaring cliffs or hidden coves, the sinewy creeks and saltmarshes of coastal Essex offer atmospheric and peaceful walking, especially at dawn and dusk or when the weather is moody. It can also feel surprisingly remote, as here at Tollesbury on the estuary of the River Blackwater near Maldon. The stories of bygone ways of life and relics of the past can be unexpected, too. From this peaceful coastal community they once fished oysters in large numbers and crewed transatlantic racing yachts for Edwardian high society; a long-vanished light railway used to run down to the pier; and a famous former light vessel has found its final berth amid the muddy channels. This easy wander around seemingly innocuous backwaters holds plenty of surprises.

Go out of the car park and turn right to walk along the road into the centre of Tollesbury, keeping straight on along the main street. Turn left at The Square, past the Kings Head pub, towards the handsome parish **church**. *Just before you get to the church is a diminutive wooden hut on the left, which turns out to be an 18th-century former lock-up for village drunks and other miscreants.*

Turn right into Church Street and go along the right-hand edge of the playing fields, turning left at the end to follow the far boundary. Go through the gap in the corner for a well-used path across fields to a lane. Turn left and follow this (Prentice

Hall Lane) down to the River Blackwater, 3km from the village. As it approaches **Rolls Farm** the lane becomes unsurfaced and finally turns into a public footpath.

Turn left on to the path that runs along the top of the embankment beside the river. Even though this isn't strictly speaking the mouth of the estuary, the river is very wide at this point. The flat and direct path is easy to follow and its modest elevation allows for good views over this flat landscape.

The 240ha Tollesbury Wick Nature Reserve is managed by Essex Wildlife Trust; and Old Hall Marshes Reserve

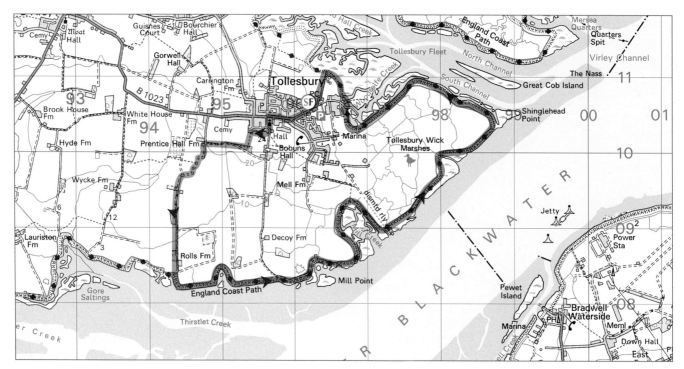

At the remains of a small pillbox at **Shinglehead Point**, 11km into the walk, the route swings round sharply and begins to head back towards Tollesbury. Across various channels and creeks to your right is the village of West Mersea on Mersea Island, the most easterly inhabited island in the UK.

Just before the point you will see what appears to be a long, low sand and shingle bank extending offshore. In fact it's part of a **beach recharge scheme** designed to protect the foreshore and saltmarsh from erosion and the land behind from flooding, but at the same time also provide new nest sites for birds like ringed plover, Little tern and oystercatcher (there's no access on to the bank during the breeding season between late April–early August). Meanwhile, landwards of the sea wall you will have noticed that the embankment is shadowed by a continuous finger of water known as a 'borrowdyke'. This is simply where the earth was dug to create the sea defence and now provides a long and sheltered ditch, usually filled with brackish water as saltwater seeps through from the estuary and mixes with freshwater.

Staying on top of the sea wall, walk alongside Tollesbury Fleet that at low tide reveals a vast network of muddy channels, creeks, pools and clumps of marsh. Some of the boats moored here, or more likely abandoned, are of dubious seaworthiness, while long and winding wooden pontoons lead often considerable distances to other vessels.

Leaving the nature reserve, continue on the fenced public footpath around the edge of **Tollesbury Marina**, past Harbour View bistro and bar, and on past a saltwater amenity lake with a miniature beach called Woodup Pool. *Tollesbury is also the berth of a distinctive, red-painted former light vessel, called Trinity, which is now a residential centre run by the Fellowship Afloat Charitable Trust.*

One of Tollesbury's most eye-catching features is its Grade II listed **sail lofts**, distinctive high-gabled wooden buildings raised on concrete piers to keep them above the high tide which floods here. They were built in the early 1900s by the Tollesbury Yacht Berthing Company, in part for local fishermen, but more particularly to house the sails of the great

(accessed via Old Hall Lane), on the far side of Tollesbury Fleet, is in the care of the RSPB. Both comprise large areas of **grazing marshes** with reedbeds, wet flushes, brackish pools and saltmarsh. Birds that breed here include bearded tit, lapwing, avocet, shelduck and shoveler, while migratory species can feature marsh harriers, curlew, sandpiper and dunlin. Small bumps in the rough pasture are likely to be ant hills belonging to the Yellow Meadow ant, which is found on the reserve, with individual mounds supporting anything up to 40,000 ants.

Approaching **Mill Point** the embankment path makes the first of two kinks inland around areas of saltmarsh and mudflats. After this you enter **Tollesbury Wick** Nature Reserve and signs ask you to keep dogs under strict control because of wildlife and grazing livestock. *In the distance is the partly decommissioned Bradwell nuclear power station. Its construction inspired Michael Morpurgo's book* Homecoming *about how an idyllic landscape of childhood memories is ruined forever.*

▲ *Pontoons on the edge of Tollesbury Fleet*

A former light vessel is among the craft moored on the creeks at Tollesbury (photo: Russell Wheeler)

J-class yachts which were owned by Edwardian high society (including Edward, Prince of Wales) and skippered by men from the village. The yachts competed in prestigious events, including *Endeavour I* which in 1934 sailed across the Atlantic as challenger for the America's Cup. Today these handsome, weather-boarded buildings are used for offices and one of them is a very handy café called The Loft (open daily except Monday).

Cross the road by the flood barrier and resume the path (waymarked the Saltmarsh Coast Trail) away from the marina and out towards Old Hall Marshes. When you come to a path junction turn left, signposted Information Hub, and follow this route back to the car park and toilets in **Tollesbury**, on the way slipping through a gap in the hedge to join a vehicle track.

All aboard the Crab and Winkle Express

A location next to the sea wall by the old pier at Tollesbury was once the terminus for the Kelvedon and Tollesbury Light Railway, known rather endearingly as the Crab and Winkle Express (there was another line nicknamed Crab and Winkle in north Kent). It opened in 1904 and the 14km route connected a number of small villages with Kelvedon, midway between Colchester and Chelmsford. Information from Mersea Museum describes how the express consisted of a tank engine pulling two carriages and a guard's van, although passengers tended to vie with crates of shellfish heading for distant markets. The line closed in 1951 and, according to the Tollesbury village website, 400 people turned out to make a final journey. Apparently on the firebox of the very last train were chalked the words 'Born 1904. Died 1951' and a note on the coal bunker warned 'there be many a poor soul have to walk [sic]'.

▲ *Tollesbury's historic sail lofts (photo: Chiz Dakin)* ▶ *Looking across the River Alde to Orford Ness (photo: Chiz Dakin)*

Walk 23
Orford

Start/Finish	Orford (quay) TM 425 495
Distance	10.25km (6.4 miles)
Total ascent	50m (170ft)
Time	3hr
Terrain	Low marshland with grassy embankments
Map	OS Explorer 212/OS Landranger 169
Refreshments	Pubs and cafés in Orford and at Orford Quay
Public transport	Bus connections to Woodbridge and Ipswich (Mon to Sat)
Parking	Riverside car park, Orford (charge)
Note	Orford Ness is open for visits on selected days, but tickets are limited so book ahead, see www.nationaltrust.org.uk/orford-ness-national-nature-reserve

For much of the 20th century a vast, bare and remote shingle spit north of Felixstowe was out of bounds to the public and a place of highly sensitive military activity. First it was used for pioneering aviation bombing techniques, ballistics testing and the development of radar, then after World War 2 top secret research into atomic bombs was carried out. Today deserted and returning to nature, Orford Ness is now managed by the National Trust and you can explore this unique time capsule following designated trails. For a wider perspective, the walk described here shadows the spit along the edge of the mainland, with close up views across the water not only of the former test sites but also the surrounding wildlife-rich marshes, islands and estuaries of this intriguing coastal landscape.

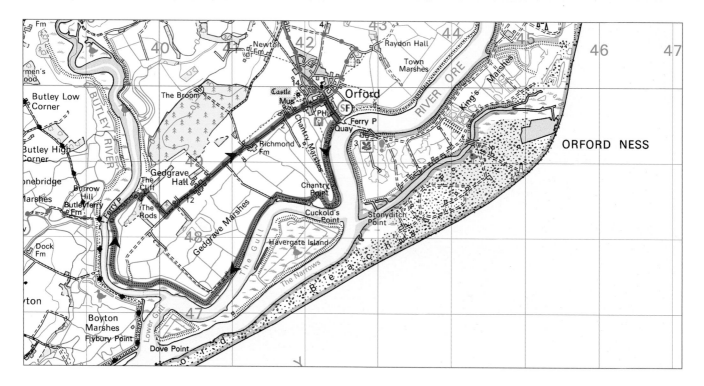

With your back to the harbour office on Orford quay, head right for the signposted path along the water's edge in front of houses. Go up a few steps and follow the popular path along the top of the embankment. There are good views of Orford Castle across the fields to the right, while the long, low form of Orford Ness fills the horizon seawards. *Orford is well known for its quality local food, such as freshly caught seafood (including oysters and crabs) and smoked fish, with a country market held every Saturday morning in the town hall.*

Continue along the obvious and easy route, past a succession of boats either moored or hauled up on the mud in various states of repair. Walk past a pillbox and where a footpath branches off to the right, go through a gate and continue ahead along the embankment top. Across the water are the odd-looking pagoda-style structures on Orford Ness.

The various buildings that you can see on Orford Ness today, many of them listed, are laboratories constructed by the **Atomic Weapons Research Establishment** from the 1950s onwards. They were used for both vibration and mechanical testing and consist of deep pits where the devices were subject to various trials involving

shaking, vibrating, extreme temperatures and excessive g-force. These were designed to check how the weapons would stand up to pressures prior to detonation and, it was claimed, never actually involved any nuclear material. Britain's very first atomic bomb (called Blue Danube) was tested here and had to be lowered into position using a 10-ton-crane. The pagoda-style reinforced concrete roofs, sitting on sturdy concrete columns, were specifically designed so that if an accident occurred a vertical blast or flying objects could be contained. Atomic testing on the site ended in 1971.

At **Chantry Point** the path swings westwards and, in the very far distance along the coast, the rows of cranes at Felixstowe Docks can be seen. A public footpath heads off inland through a gate, beside which a notice confirms that the embankment route beyond here is a permissive path to Butley Ferry and requests that dogs should be on a lead.

Stay on top of the high and grassy sea wall. Just across the water is Havergate Island, which claims to be Suffolk's only true island.

▲ *Pagoda-style buildings on Orford Ness were once used for weapons testing (photo: Chiz Dakin)*

has opted not to build up the sea walls but in fact to lower them as part of a natural flood management approach, using sluices to carefully control the amount of water in or out, which also helps regulate salinity levels.

Carry on around the edge of **Gedgrave Marshes**, a tranquil place but for the general cacophony of gulls, geese and other birdlife. Follow the edge of the Butley River as it heads inland, over two stiles and 6km after leaving Orford Quay arrive at Butley Ferry. *Butley Ferry is run by volunteers from the Alde and Ore Association who row visitors across on summer weekends (subject to availability and weather conditions).*

Continue along the riverside until finally waymarks point right, away from the water, past some buildings that include a working smokehouse. Follow the sandy drive that twists and turns its way across the fields. The modest elevation allows good views back over the marshes towards Havergate Island and Orford Ness. *Designated in 1970, the Suffolk Coast & Heaths Area of Outstanding Natural Beauty stretches for 250km^2 (155 square miles) and encompasses both Orford and Dunwich (Walk 24).*

Stay on the farm track, which after **Gedgrave Hall** becomes a surfaced lane. This leads all the way back to Orford, with the giant keep of Orford Castle directly ahead. At the end of the lane either turn left for the castle and village centre; or go right, and at the end of this right again, to return to the start at **Orford quay**.

Henry II ordered work to begin on **Orford Castle** in 1165 as part of his plans to develop a new port and provide extra defence against invasions on the east coast. Although silting and erosion caused the port to decline, the castle remained a royal stronghold for over 150 years until 1336 when King Edward III sold it to Robert of Ufford, Earl of Suffolk. It has a highly unusual and very well-preserved polygonal keep, as well as lower and upper halls, chapel, kitchen, various passages and chambers. Perhaps best of all, you can climb all the way to the roof from where there are superb views across the coast and in particular the full length of Orford Ness. From here you can really appreciate the sheer size of the ness and the almost bewildering array of structures dotted about it.

Havergate has been an RSPB nature reserve since 1949 after avocets, previously extinct in the UK for over a century, were found breeding on the island. Not long after this the handsome wading bird was chosen to feature on the organisation's logo; but Havergate is also well known for other birds like spoonbill and common terns and it has a large gull colony. Over recent years the low-lying island has suffered from tidal storm surges which has affected the saltwater lagoons, marshes and shingle banks which provide the birds with nesting habitat. In response, the RSPB

From wilderness to warfare (and back again)

National Trust warning sign on Orford Ness

Although there are similarities with Dungeness (Walk 20), the physical separation of Orford Ness from the mainland and the fact that it was entirely closed to the public for so many years makes it truly unique. There's an odd juxtaposition between this wild and windswept shingle spit, a national nature reserve that's home to rare plants and birds, and the secretive world of surveillance and destructive modern weaponry. Now, at last, you can explore this almost surreal environment, although you have to follow waymarked trails, some of which are closed in the bird-breeding season. However, the main 8km route is permanently open and leads across to the far shore by the lighthouse. On the way you can look inside various bunkers, control rooms and lookout towers, all with excellent interpretation. It's easy to spend several hours wandering about and because visitor numbers are limited you can enjoy some solitude – which, despite all that's happened here, is what Orford Ness is all about.

Walberswick and Dunwich

Start/Finish	Walberswick (Cliff Field car park) TM 500 746
Distance	18km (11 miles)
Total ascent	140m (460ft)
Time	4hr 30min
Terrain	Generally firm paths through woods, heath and marshes, long stretch of shingle and sandy beach
Map	OS Explorer 231/OS Landranger 156
Refreshments	Pubs in Walberswick and Dunwich, tearooms in Walberswick, Dunwich and Dunwich Heath
Public transport	None
Parking	Cliff Field car park, Walberswick (charge)
Note	Dogs on lead around nature reserves and on heath

Nowhere is the impact of climate change and rising sea levels more keenly felt than on England's east coast. Whereas Spurn Head (Walk 26) is being re-shaped today, in low-lying Suffolk the sea has simply wiped out most traces of one of England's leading medieval settlements and fishing ports. Dunwich village museum tells the story of how a whole town once stretched out beyond the shingle bank, a victim of storms, silting and relentless coastal erosion. Walberswick harbour has also been re-fashioned; Minsmere Cliffs are fenced off as they crumble away; and the freshwater Dingle Marshes are gradually succumbing to saltwater invasion. This is an instructive and quite easy outing through a variety of habitats, with the inevitable conclusion that in the long run, the battle between land and sea has only one winner.

From the car park at Walberswick, walk through to the beach via a short boardwalk. Turn right and go along the shore for 500 metres, then turn right on the first of two public footpaths across the marshes. Go over a footbridge and turn left to walk beside **Dunwich River**, keeping left at a fork. At the brick stump of an old windmill turn left on to a wider path along the top of the embankment above the reedbeds.

At a fork go right, away from the sea towards scrub and woodland, and follow the obvious route via a small plantation and along the edge of **Dunwich Forest** on a wide sandy track past occasional buildings. There are intermittent views across Dingle Marshes toward the sea.

After 5.5km you finally reach a road. Turn left and follow this past the church and into the small village of **Dunwich**, with its museum and pub (The Ship).

At the bend, just after the pub car park, take the narrow public footpath directly ahead that climbs into a small copse. Follow this past the remains of the friary on your right, which you can access from the path. *Greyfriars Monastery was established by Franciscan monks who first settled at Dunwich in the 1250s, and its surviving fragments give some indication of the size and scale of this once-wealthy institution.*

Continue to the path junction at the far end and go straight on into Greyfriars Wood, bending right to follow a ditch and underneath a curious little bridge among the trees. Go straight on until you reach a road at a bend.

After a few paces turn left, down a private drive (public footpath), and at the end continue along a woodland path to reach another road. Go straight over for a wide heathland track until you reach a crossroads of routes. Turn left for a clear and direct footpath that heads across the middle of **Dunwich Heath** to the clifftop to the far side, where former coastguard cottages

◀ *Deserted coastline at Walberswick (photo: Chiz Dakin)*

are now used by the National Trust for a tearoom, toilets and **information centre**.

In terms of disappearing natural habitats, East Anglia is probably best known for its once prolific swamp and marshland known as the Fens, but another (and in some ways its antithesis) is **coastal lowland heathland**. Dry, sandy and dominated by ling, bell heather and gorse, it once stretched from Ipswich to Lowestoft, but incursion by woodland and our insatiable appetite for farming improvement, building and development has reduced the Sandlings (as it was known) to a few isolated pockets, such as here at Dunwich Heath. This location has been in the care of the National Trust for over 50 years who actively manage it for rare heathland wildlife, such as nightjar, Dartford warbler, adder, slow worm, mining bee and lacewing insects called ant-lions.

▲   *The beach at Dunwich (photo: Chiz Dakin)*

Walk through the car park and to the top edge of the slope. Below you are the reedbeds, lagoons and woodland of Minsmere Nature Reserve, and beyond that the rather jarring shapes of Sizewell nuclear power station. *Minsmere is one of the RSPB's flagship reserves and its extensive reedbeds are famous for rare birds such as bittern and marsh harrier.*

There are two choices for a return walking route to Dunwich. The most direct (3km) is along the shore below the low cliffs. The top of the shingle beach is above the high water mark and is safe to walk, albeit rather hard going underfoot after a while. However, as the tide falls there is a continuous sandy strip further down the shingle that offers much firmer and pleasant walking. Alternatively, from the coastguard cottages follow a waymarked path northwards along the top of Minsmere Cliffs. This then joins a lane and you can pick up the outward route back to Dunwich.

From the large beachside car park at Dunwich walk along the firm and part-vegetated landward side of the dunes, with good views across Dingle Marshes Nature Reserve.

Like Minsmere, the wetland immediately south of Walberswick is part of the wider Suffolk Coast National Nature Reserve and is prized for its mix of freshwater and coastal habitats. The slightly salty (or brackish) pools of **Dingle Marshes** attract ducks and waders like wigeon and redshank, while the extensive reedbeds are often busy with bearded tits and warblers. If you visit early or late in the day you may also be treated to the sight of a marsh harrier,

Ruins of Greyfriars Monastery at Dunwich (photo: Chiz Dakin)

gliding low and effortlessly across the reeds. The marshes are separated from the sea by a mile-long shingle bank, but there have been regular breaches in recent years and, despite subsequent repairs, it seems likely that history will one day repeat itself and the sea will eventually reclaim more of this vulnerable Suffolk coast.

When you come to a fenced-off area, designed to protect nesting ringed plover and Little terns, which lay their eggs on shallow scrapes on the open beach, return to the shore and follow this all the way back to Walberswick beach. If you want to extend the walk via the village continue to the mouth of the River Blyth and follow this up to the harbour and ferry, and then head back through **Walberswick.** *A daily foot ferry across the River Blyth allows access to Southwold, home to the renowned Adnams brewery whose beers have nautical names such as Broadside, Ghost Ship and Lighthouse.*

▲ *Sea kale growing on the beach below Dunwich Cliffs (photo: Chiz Dakin)*

Disappearing Dunwich

It's very hard to stand on the empty beach at Dunwich today and imagine a prosperous medieval town stretching out for over 1.6km into (what is now) the North Sea, but a thousand years ago this was the case. Dunwich was one of the most important towns in late Saxon and Norman times, boasting a large harbour and fishing fleet of 70 boats, as well as numerous churches and a bishopric that took in all of East Anglia. But the tenth largest settlement in England was literally washed away by a series of devastating storms, surges and floods that took place between 1286 and 1347. All that's left are the ruins of a Franciscan friary on the cliff edge and the chapel of the Leper Hospital beside the present-day church. To learn more about the remarkable story make sure to visit the outstanding Dunwich Museum, which is open daily between April and October.

Walk 25

Burnham Deepdale to Sheringham

Start	Burnham Deepdale (Deepdale Café) TF 803 443
Finish	Sheringham (promenade) TG 159 435
Distance	49.5km (30.7 miles)
Total ascent	85m (290ft)
Time	11hr
Terrain	Firm embankment paths, tracks, sandy beach and shingle banks
Map	OS Explorer 251 & 252/OS Landranger 132 & 133
Refreshments	Cafés and pubs at regular intervals, including Burnham Deepdale, Burnham Overy Staithe, Holkham, Wells, Stiffkey, Blakeney, Cley, Weybourne and Sheringham
Public transport	The Coasthopper bus provides frequent daily services along the entire coast path
Parking	Roadside at Burnham Deepdale, car parks at Sheringham (charge)
Note	This is a 2-day walk from Burnham Deepdale to Stiffkey (24km/15 miles) and Stiffkey to Sheringham (25.5km/16 miles), but a good bus service makes any variation possible

Walking the coast of north Norfolk is big picture stuff. Of course, there are fine details like the traditional flint buildings, windmills and birdlife, but in this largely flat landscape of yawning skies and wide horizons the interplay of land and sky, and in particular the effect of light on the broad sweep of marsh, mudflat, sand and water can be mesmerising. Route finding is relatively easy, conditions underfoot (shingle notwithstanding) straightforward, so it's a walk where you can focus on the entire canvas – or perhaps, in a nice way, choose not to focus at all. Even better, the Norfolk Coast Path is well served by regular daily buses, so this 2-day walk can be adapted to suit individual distances or accommodation choices, including extending the walk either end to Brancaster and Cromer.

Day 1

At Burnham Deepdale cross the road opposite Deepdale Café for the signposted coast path out to the edge of the saltmarsh (the waymarking along the entire National Trail is very good). Turn right and follow the obvious path along the embankment for 6.3km to **Burnham Overy Staithe**. *The pub at Burnham Overy Staithe is called The Hero in honour of Admiral Nelson, he of the Battle of Trafalgar fame, who was born in nearby Burnham Thorpe.*

Walk through the village and down to the quayside, then out, once more, on the embankment path to reach the broad sandy sweep of **Holkham Bay**. Turn right and follow this delightful stretch (paddling if conditions allow) for over 3km, but be aware that a section of beach is a designated naturist zone. There are discreet signs announcing this, but some of the users of the beach may not be so modest.

Where the edge of the beach draws back and the pine trees converge, veer right to reach **Holkham Gap**. The Lookout

centre has information about Holkham National Nature Reserve, as well as offering toilets and refreshments.

The Norfolk coast has plenty of well-heeled pubs and fashionable bistros, but you can still enjoy the **fruits of the sea** relatively cheaply and directly. Kiosks on the quayside at Wells dispense whelks and cockles in small polystyrene tubs, as well as huge quantities of fish and chips. Look out for bunches of freshly cut marsh samphire (cooked and eaten like asparagus) on sale from some roadside properties along the coast; and at the renowned smokehouse at Cley you can buy smoked mackerel, eel, shell-on prawns and kiln-roasted salmon. The tidal creeks around Brancaster are famous for their tender mussels; and of course there are the sweet-tasting crabs of Cromer, just beyond the end this walk, which feed off a chalk reef just off the coast and are available in April and May.

Now follow signs for Wells-next-the-Sea along a wide track running landwards of a broad strip of pines, known as Holkham Meals, to emerge by a car park, café and caravan park at the end of Beach Road (the beach itself is behind the trees to your left). Turn right by the new **lifeboat station** and walk along the top of the embankment into **Wells-next-the-Sea**, with a vast area of saltmarsh opposite across the narrow channel. *The town's tall and distinctive quayside landmark, with its elaborate gantry, is called The Granary and was built to aid the export of local malt for the brewing trade (it's now luxury flats).*

Leave the town on the quayside heading east, past the Port of Wells Lobster Hatchery building and boatyards, and back out to the embankment path alongside Warham Marsh for 4.7km to reach the National Trust's **Stiffkey Greenway** car park. If you are ending day one here turn right for Stiffkey village and bus stop.

Day 2

The coast path continues its uncomplicated and peaceful passage eastwards along the edge of the saltmarsh all the way to **Morston**, where there is a seasonal National Trust refreshment kiosk and toilets; and then on to the village of **Blakeney**.

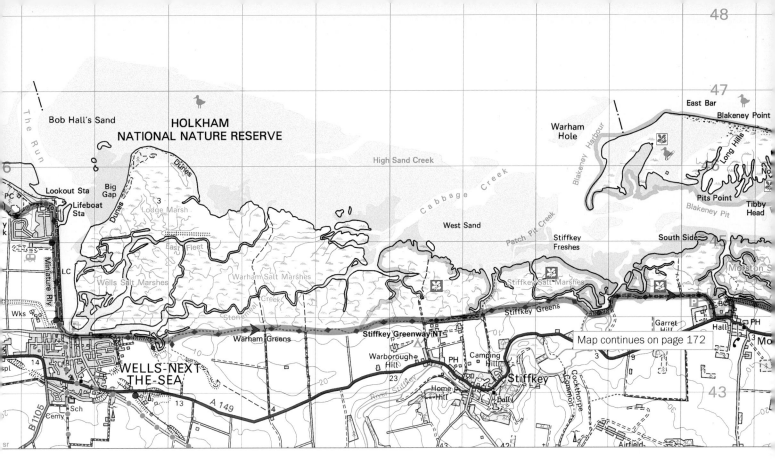

The sand and shingle spit of **Blakeney Point** reaches back along the coastline in the shape of a giant claw. It's a location rich in wildlife and a draw for many visitors, but the National Trust restricts public access to the far western side of this national nature reserve as it's home to Britain's largest colony of grey seals. Although they can be seen all year around, the adults (which can weigh up to 250kg each) begin congregating in earnest from October and over 3000 pups are now born here each winter, which is not bad considering that the colony is only 20 years old. The best way of seeing the seals close-up is to take a boat trip on one of the licensed operators from the quays at Morston and Blakeney.

The coast path now does another loop, this time for 4km around Fresh Marshes in order to reach **Cley next the Sea**. Follow the narrow road through the village centre, past the deli, smokehouse and gallery, then look for the coast path sign that takes you round the back of the buildings via the windmill and out alongside the road to reach the shore at **Cley Eye**. Here turn

right for a 6km walk along the very direct shingle embankment above the waves. In places you can take to the semi-vegetated rear of the shingle bank, which makes for firmer conditions

▲ *Some of the coast path follows the shingle beach*   171

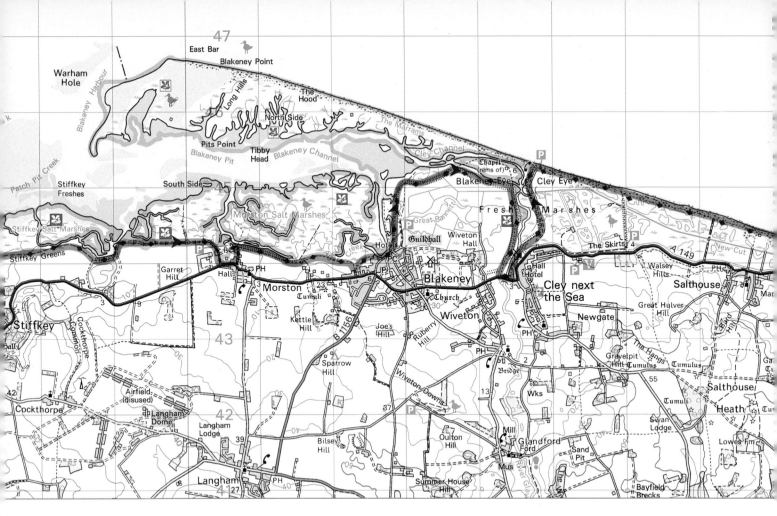

underfoot, but it can be slow going. *The high shingle bank forms part of the sea defences along this low-lying stretch of coast and it's not unusual to see bulldozers rebuilding it after winter storms.*

Approaching Weybourne Hope the walking gets easier; and beyond the car park and toilets the ground rises and the path takes to the grassy top of low and undulating cliffs. Follow this obvious and well-walked route alongside a golf course and all the way to finish at the small holiday resort of **Sheringham** (Cromer is a further 7.2km further on).

Birdwatching on the Norfolk coast

To say that the Norfolk coast is rich in birdlife is like saying London has a few red buses. There is a string of internationally important nature reserves along this short stretch of coast – Titchwell Marsh, Scolt Head, Blakeney, Holkham, Cley – where, depending on the time of year, you can see a wide variety of wildfowl, waders and sea birds, as well as huge flock of wintering geese. Although early morning or evening, especially on the marshes, is generally considered the active time for most birds, you may even spot a star species like a marsh harrier quartering the reedbeds in the middle of the day. It's partly to do with the varied habitat of the Norfolk coast, from sand and shingle beaches to saltmarsh, reeds, mudflats and lagoons, but also because it's on the flight path of many migrating coastal birds. Although you can see much from the coast path, it's worth a short diversion to one of the excellent visitor centres, such as Cley Marshes (Norfolk Wildlife Trust) or Titchwell (RSPB).

Open shoreline towards Weybourne

Aerial view of Spurn Head (photo: David Nichols/Yorkshire Wildlife Trust, Walk 26)

North East

The Wash to the Scottish border

Nowhere is the dynamism of the English coast more in evidence than along Lincolnshire's soft, low and vulnerable shoreline, where the ability to swiftly realign the England Coast Path in response to further and inevitable erosion is already proving useful. At the mouth of the Humber you can see for yourself how the sea appears to be actively changing Spurn Head from a sandy spit into a tidal island (Walk 26). Yorkshire Wildlife Trust's excellent visitor centre also explains how Spurn is a vital location for birds, especially for migrants on a passage along the east coast.

Further north the coast rises up more defiantly, with the prominent chalk cliffs of Flamborough Head dominating the view from Bridlington. Walk 27 goes on to finish at the 122m-high Bempton Cliffs and the mesmerising spectacle of

thousands of noisy sea birds, but although the clifftop path is high it's also mostly level, as well as safe and easy to follow.

This transition for walkers from low-level shoreline to elevated clifftop continues beyond Scarborough, another traditional and attractive English seaside resort, where the well-walked route follows the Cleveland Way National Trail. The glorious 2-day coastal outing to Staithes (Walk 28) takes in everything from high cliffs and sandy bays to an historic port that launched explorations to the New World; but in places the path is also exposed and undulating, with challenge and adventure.

Although there are pockets of the north east coast that are highly developed, especially around the mouths of the Tees and Tyne, elsewhere the changing face of industry is allowing nature to return – and with it some fantastic coastal walking opportunities. The County Durham shore between Seaham and Hartlepool (Walk 29) was once black with coal waste, but when the pits closed the clear-up began, and now the gentle clifftop meadows and wooded denes are increasingly alive with plants and wildlife.

For most visitors, the temperature of the North Sea is not usually conducive to swimming, but beach-walking with the occasional paddle can be a real treat. North of Craster (Walk 30) the peaceful Northumberland coastline is characterised by a series of gentle sandy bays and long open beaches, so that (wildlife and tide/weather considerations notwithstanding) you can follow the water's edge for long stretches. Along the way a series of dramatic clifftop castles almost act as markers. The relative remoteness of this coast keeps crowds to a minimum – which is all the more reason to reach for your boots.

▲ *Chalk cliffs at Dykes End near South Landing (Walk 27)*   ▶ *An eroded roadway on Spurn Head*

Walk 26
Spurn Head

Start/Finish	Kilnsea (Blue Bell car park) TA 417 158
Distance	13.25km (8.2 miles)
Total ascent	10m (30ft)
Time	3hr 30min
Terrain	Sand and shingle beach, low vegetated dunes
Map	OS Explorer 292/OS Landranger 113
Refreshments	Blue Bell Café at Spurn Discovery Centre (open daily), Crown & Anchor Inn, Kilnsea
Public transport	None
Parking	Blue Bell car park (charge) or Spurn Discovery Centre car park (charge)
Note	Spurn Head is free to access on foot, but dogs are not allowed in order to protect the sensitive wildlife and habitats
Warning	Check the tide times before you set off as the Wash Over section can be impassable at very high tides. Go to www.ywt.org.uk/nature-reserves/spurn-national-nature-reserve or see the noticeboard in the Discovery Centre car park.

Curving out into the mouth of the Humber like a crooked finger, the pencil-thin sand and shingle spit of Spurn Head provides a truly unique coastal walk full of unexpected surprises. Whether you're a birdwatcher or military historian, geographer or devotee of lighthouses, this flat and comparatively short there-and-back is utterly absorbing – and that's not counting the picnic on the beach examining fossils or watching the busy shipping. Spurn Head also provides the storyline of how the shape and look of the English east coast is ever-changing in the face of rising sea levels and extreme weather events. Now periodically cut off by very high tides, walk over to Spurn Head while you still can.

From the car park turn left at the crossroads by the former Blue Bell café. Walk down the lane towards Spurn Head and call in at Yorkshire Wildlife Trust's **Spurn Discovery Centre**. *The elegant modern visitor centre, curved and wooden-clad, stands on gabions filled with recycled rock, allowing the centre to withstand floods to which this vulnerable coastline is especially prone.*

Continue along the road, past the barrier, and as the land narrows walk out across the **Wash Over**. On the far side is higher ground and here a level, sandy vehicle track runs the full length of the spit, amid the grass-topped dunes and low vegetation. Walk past the **High Tide Shelter** (a small wooden shed) for 1.2km until you reach a waymarked grassy path off to the right signposted Natural Heritage Trail. Follow this wide and easy route through the dunes and cropped grass of Chalk Bank past a series of publicly accessible bird hides, plus a Heligoland trap used to ring and record birds. Beyond the trap follow public footpath signs through an area once used by the lifeboatmen and

▲   *The High Tide Shelter for those who mis-time their visit*

coastguards as allotments (known as the Potato Fields) until you re-join the road near the lighthouse.

Arriving at the **lighthouse** just over 5km from the start, you can go inside for a visit either now or on the way back. Continue along the road to the lifeboat station and Wildlife Trust base (toilets). At the very far side of these buildings follow the waymarked path around to the left, across scrub, keeping the former VTS (Vessel Traffic Service) base, with its radar and satellite dishes, over to the left beyond a small grazed paddock. The route reaches an old gun emplacement, the roof of which has been turned into a handy viewing platform.

Spurn Head's strategic position at the mouth of the Humber has seen it fortified since Napoleonic times, although the gun emplacements here date from World War 2. It has also meant that warning lights for shipping have been lit or have shone continuously for several centuries. The black-and-white striped lighthouse so prominent today stands 38m high and remains the tallest in northern England. When operational, its beam had a reach of 27km.

Following its decommission in 1985 it has been turned into a fascinating visitor centre and there are terrific views across the whole of Spurn Head from the lantern room at the top, as well as further afield to the Lincolnshire Wolds, Grimsby, Cleethorpes and upstream towards Kingston upon Hull. The lighthouse is usually open Friday to Sunday and some weekdays in the summer holidays.

About 50 metres beyond the gun battery turn right for a waymarked route through a dense thicket and past a former searchlight bunker partly hidden in the bushes and dwarf trees. Eventually the path emerges on the beach at the far end of the spit. *Roughly 2.5km offshore in the mouth of the Humber is Bull Sand Fort, a World War 1 concrete defence built with great difficulty and ultimately little purpose.*

After taking in the wide-ranging views and busy shipping lanes (with the huge vessels passing alarmingly close) turn right and walk along the sandy beach back round towards the lifeboat station. Go under the jetty and at the end of a high section of sea wall clamber up the sandy bank to re-join the road.

Humber Lifeboat was established in 1810 and is the only RNLI lifeboat station in the UK with a full-time crew.

Turn left and walk back along the road towards the mainland. Immediately before the lighthouse go right on a waymarked path which weaves its way along the crest of the undulating dunes, behind the lighthouse, on the eastern side of the spit. Eventually it drops back down to the road. You can either follow this back to the **Wash Over** or alternatively walk along the beach on the seaward side of the spit.

In spring and autumn Spurn Head is a great location to watch **birds in migration**. Thousands pass along the coast and rarities are sometimes blown off course, which in the past have included such unusual visitors as a bee-eater and an albatross. In winter there are large flocks of brent geese and waders like dunlin and knot, many hundreds and sometimes thousands strong. The range of habitats on and around this sliver of land also include grassland and scrub, so that birds like stonechats, warblers and whitethroats can be found in the summer undergrowth. Spurn Discovery Centre has advice on what to see and the best places to see them.

If it's safe to do so, walk back across the Wash Over and unless you want to return along the road to visit the Discovery Centre for refreshments or more information, continue ahead along the beach until you reach the car park and the start of the walk near **Kilnsea**.

The 'wash over' section now succumbs to the sea at very high tides

Sandy spit or tidal island?

In December 2013 Spurn Head was overrun by a powerful storm surge which washed away the road and sea defences at the narrowest point of the spit, barely 150 metres wide. Since then, this exposed section of beach (now called the Wash Over) becomes submerged and impassable at very high tides. It has meant that Spurn Head, which is basically a narrow peninsula consisting of sand and shingle banks bound together by marram grass and sea buckthorn, has effectively become Britain's newest tidal island. Given the fragility of the spit and the dynamic force of the North Sea and bad weather, there are no plans to restore the breach; and in fact it simply represents the latest in Spurn's ever-changing position. For many centuries, the combination of storms and longshore drift has steadily moved sand and silt along the Holderness coast, so that Spurn's shape has constantly altered. Breaches in the spit have occurred before; and in medieval times there was even a small port on sandbanks off Spurn Head that rivalled Hull and Grimsby, but it has long since been washed away and no traces remain.

Flamborough Head

Start	Bridlington (North Promenade) TA 193 678
Finish	Bempton TA 191 721
Distance	19km (11.8 miles)
Total ascent	595m (1950ft)
Time	4hr 15min
Terrain	Clifftop path, generally firm and level, some short but sharp ascents and descents
Map	OS Explorer 301 Scarborough, Bridlington & Flamborough Head/OS Landranger 101
Refreshments	Cafés or pubs at Bridlington, Flamborough, Selwicks Bay, Thornwick Bay and the RSPB Seabird Centre near Bempton
Public transport	Weekday buses between Bempton, Flamborough and Bridlington, regular trains between Bempton and Bridlington
Parking	Numerous car parks at Bridlington (charge)

There's something irresistible about a big, bold headland, the way that it juts out confidently into the sea and how it almost seems to draw your boots towards it. Flamborough Head is certainly one such place. Northern England's only chalk sea cliffs form an impressive 10km promontory and become seriously high around Bempton where they shriek and reek with birdlife, while elsewhere they're peppered with dramatic arches, stacks and blowholes. The clifftop path is firm underfoot and mostly level and obvious, plus there are bus and train connections that allow for a linear outing. With far-reaching views, hidden ravines and coves, plus a traditional fish and chip supper awaiting you on your return at Bridlington, it's a tasty day out on the mouth-watering North Yorkshire coast.

At the far end of Bridlington's North Promenade (Lime Kiln Lane) follow the very popular path up on to the low clifftop and past **Sewerby** with its elegant Hall, then skirt a cricket green and golf course. The number of visitors out for a short stroll

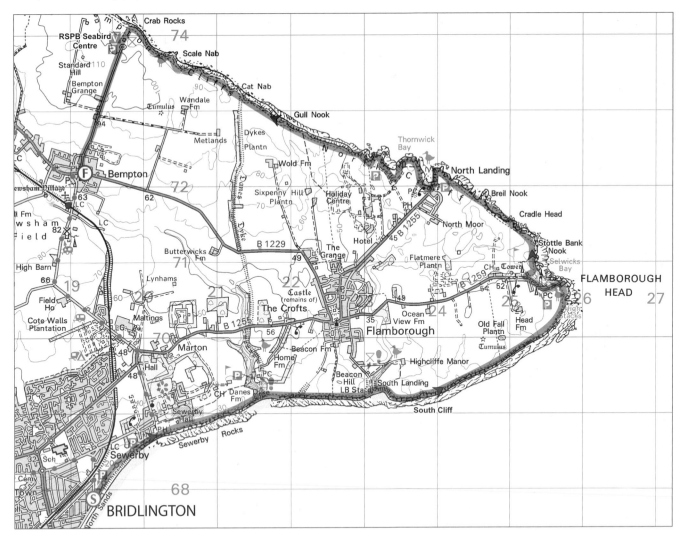

Cliffs at Selwicks Bay (photo: Chiz Dakin)

The cliff formation known as the Drinking Dinosaur at Flamborough Head (photo: Chiz Dakin)

gradually subsides as the path veers inland to a junction of tracks at **Danes Dyke**, a local nature reserve named after an ancient ditch and bank earthwork which runs across the entire headland. Turn right and descend the wooded path to emerge at a small rocky beach.

The route clambers back up on to the clifftop opposite, resuming its easy passage along field edges, with broadening views across the bay back to Bridlington and the long, low coast of Holderness beyond. In the far distance is the Humber Estuary and the Lincolnshire Wolds.

Arriving at **South Landing** after 5km, the path drops down to Flamborough lifeboat station where there is a wide slipway at a natural break in the cliffs. *Until 1938 there were two lifeboats stationed at Flamborough, on either side of the headland, in case the prevailing weather prevented one from being launched.*

Go up a series of steps behind a parking area and follow the path along the top of **South Cliff**, making for the distinctive white lighthouse at the tip of the headland. Look out for kestrels which appear to thrive along this stretch.

The tip (or should that be nose?) of **Flamborough Head** is dominated by a handsome, white-painted lighthouse, with a separate fog signal station on the clifftop nearby. This is the midway point of the walk, about 8km from Bridlington.

When viewed from across Bridlington Bay the rigid point of **Flamborough Head** dominates the horizon. No wonder that some believe the name, spelt Fleneburg in the Domesday Book, might possibly derive from the Saxon Flaen meaning a dart. The present lighthouse was built in 1806 and stands 26.5m tall. However, located further back, amid the buildings of Flamborough village, are the remains of a recently restored octagonal chalk tower that was built as long ago as 1674 as a light tower. Passing ships were supposed to pay a tax according to the weight of their cargo so that a fire could be kept burning at its top, but so few bothered to pay that the owner went bankrupt and the lighthouse never served its intended purpose.

Despite the myriad small paths simply follow the edge of the cliff around the headland, looking down on to numerous arches and caves, and make your way past the lighthouse, café

and car park. Now heading northwards, walk along the outer edge of a golf course and along the level clifftop peppered with holes and depressions where the chalk has succumbed to the sea. They have evocative names like Stottle Bank Nook, Cradle Head and Breil Nook. Enter Yorkshire Wildlife Trust's Flamborough Cliffs reserve and follow the path all the way to **North Landing**, where there's a café and toilets.

The path continues from the far end of the large car park and soon rounds another promontory to reach **Thornwick Bay**, passing landwards of a couple of houses on the edge of the eroding cliff. A well-used path runs down to the sheltered sandy cove, where a deep and narrow crack in the cliffs, known as Thornwick Hole, leads to a cave.

The coast of Yorkshire and north east England is associated with a traditional type of open fishing boat called a **coble**. It has a distinctive high bow and shallow keel so that it can be launched off beaches or places where there is no proper harbour, such as at North Landing. Here the boats are dragged up and down the shore (today by tractor but formerly by hand) and to assist their smooth passage small logs known as 'fearton trees' are placed underneath the vessel to act as rollers. The name apparently comes from 'a foot and three', which was the original length of the logs. In 1880 there were as many as 80 cobles fishing from North Landing, but today just a few remain, mostly catching lobster and crab or taking visitors out fishing or birdwatching.

Unless you want to visit the beach, walk along the tarmac drive out to Thornwick Café, then head left, away from the sea, to follow a narrow path around the edge of a caravan park. Soon the open fields return and the purposeful route strides along **North Cliff**. *From October to February sea anglers fish for cod from the top of these 60m sheer cliffs, using sturdy rods and poles with lines over 270 metres long.*

There are now far-reaching views ahead towards Filey Brigg and the higher cliffs beyond, where the North York Moors roll down to the sea. More immediately the chalk cliffs beneath your feet are getting sterner and eventually rise up to 122m. As you enter the RSPB's Bempton Cliffs reserve there are more and more seabirds, best admired from one of several wooden

viewing platforms where you can look down on thousands of noisy gannets, fulmars, kittiwakes and puffins.

At a footpath sign for Bempton turn left for a short, surfaced path to the **Seabird Centre**, where there's a café and toilets; or you can venture further along the cliff path to visit other viewing platforms.

To finish the walk follow the lane from the Seabird Centre for 1.6km into the village of Bempton, from where there is a bus and train service back to Bridlington.

Gannets, gulls and other noisy birds

It's not until, from the safety of a viewing platform, you peer over the edge of Bempton Cliffs that you realise what all the fuss is about. Nothing quite prepares you for the sight, sound and smell of tens of thousands of seabirds. Some sit on narrow ledges on the cliffs, others form rafts out to sea, but many simply wheel endlessly off the face of the soaring cliffs. The noise is startling, sometimes deafening, and depending on where you stand and the wind direction it can also assault your sense of smell. The RSPB estimates that up to a quarter of a million birds are present at Bempton Cliffs between March and October, including large numbers of guillemot, puffin, razorbill, shag and fulmar, as well as England's largest mainland breeding colony of gannets. There's more information at the RSPB's Seabird Centre (open daily, year-round) which during the summer also features a live webcam of the birds on their cliff-ledge nests.

▲ *Boats at North Landing (photo: Chiz Dakin)*

Scarborough to Staithes

Start	Scarborough (North Bay) TA 035 908
Finish	Staithes (harbour) NZ 783 188
Distance	50.5km (31.4 miles)
Total ascent	2025m (6640ft)
Time	12hr
Terrain	High and often undulating clifftop, bays and beaches, some steep and rough sections
Map	OS Outdoor Leisure 27 North York Moors Eastern area/OS Landranger 94 & 101
Refreshments	Cafés, shops and pubs at numerous points along the route, including Ravenscar, Boggle Hole, Robin Hood's Bay, Whitby, Sandsend, Runswick Bay, Port Mulgrave and Staithes
Public transport	Daily buses between Scarborough, Robin Hood's Bay, Whitby and Staithes
Parking	Car parks in all main locations (mainly charge)
Note	This is a 2-day walk (Scarborough to Whitby, 31.75km/19.7 miles, Whitby to Staithes, 18.75km/11.7 miles) or for a more relaxed 3-day outing stop first at Boggle Hole or Robin Hood's Bay and then Whitby
Warning	A small section of the beach path at Runswick Bay is occasionally impassable for a short period at high tide

Whitby harbour, with the abbey on the headland

These days we walk the coast for recreation and adventure, but in the 1700s that sense of discovery was more about what lay beyond the flat blue horizon. Yorkshire lad James Cook spent his early years in Staithes and Whitby, learning his trade before taking to the sea and carving out a career that would see him sail round the world several times on ground-breaking voyages and 'discover' Australia and New Zealand. The world seems a much smaller and less mysterious place these days, but as you stride the swashbuckling cliffs of North Yorkshire and gaze out to sea, just imagine what it must have been like to simply not know what was out there. This is a superb but mostly high-level walking route, sometimes exposed and with a few steep slopes, but there are plenty of facilities along the way so take your time and savour the experience.

Day 1

The walk begins near **Scalby Mills** at the far end of Scarborough's **North Bay**. The path, which is often sign-posted as the Cleveland Way, follows an obvious and relatively easy route along the level clifftop. However, at **Hayburn Wyke** the trail plunges temporarily into the steep wooded mouth of Hayburn Beck, before resuming the open field edges along the clifftop on the far side.

After 14.5km you arrive at **Ravenscar** to pass inland of **Raven Hall** (a hotel) via a short pavement section. Take the downhill track past the National Trust's visitor centre and café, following signs for the alum works. Continue across fields and via a lane to eventually reach **Boggle Hole** youth hostel, where the Quarterdeck Café is open to the public.

Today **Ravenscar** is little more than a village, boasting a few houses, a hotel and a couple of cafés, but at the turn of the 20th century developers earmarked the prominent clifftop site for a brand new seaside resort to rival neighbouring Scarborough. The railway line had arrived a few years before, and now

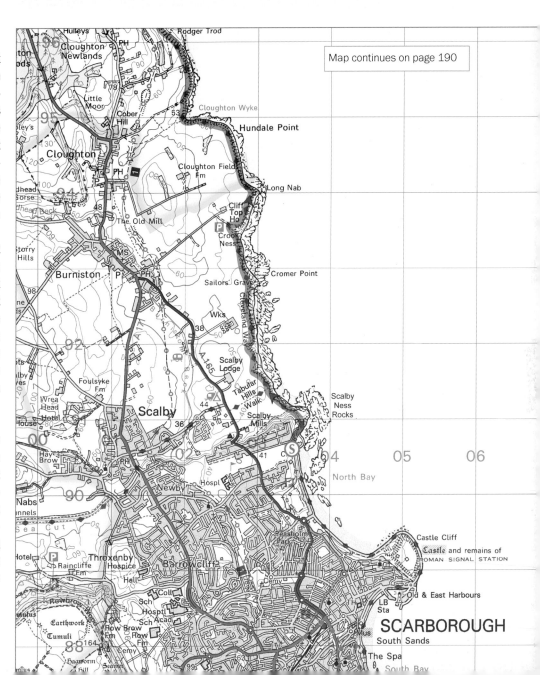

Map continues on page 190

Map continues on page 192

new roads were laid out, drains dug and a mains water supply established. Several villas were built and the foundations prepared for others, but the developers' dreams were not shared by enough investors and in 1913 the bubble burst and the company went bankrupt. It was thought that the site was too isolated and exposed, perhaps too far from the beach, so the new town provisionally called The Peak never materialised.

From Boggle Hole it's a short beach walk to the settlement of **Robin Hood's Bay**, of if the tide is high follow the track across the clifftop instead. *Robin Hood's Bay is where Wainwright's Coast to Coast Walk finishes, having begun its long journey on the Cumbrian coast at St Bees (Walk 1).*

With your back to the slipway head up the old town's main street (arguably its only street) and follow this steeply up to the modern houses at the very top. Continue past the car park and guest houses and turn right into Mount Pleasant North. The path resumes at the far end and from here it's an obvious, well-walked and gently undulating route along the clifftop all the way to **Whitby** (just under 11km). Approaching the town, the coast path goes through the middle of a caravan park (follow the signposts) and arrives at the ruined **abbey** on the hilltop above the harbour. Whitby Youth Hostel is next to the abbey. Walk through the churchyard of St Mary's and down the famous 199 steps into the town, turning left at the bottom to thread your way through the shops to the swing bridge over the harbour.

Near Port Mulgrave

On a sunny summer's day, when Whitby is thronging with tourists, it's maybe a little hard to see why the Victorian novelist **Bram Stoker** chose Whitby as one of the settings for his classic Gothic novel *Dracula*. But even in 1890 this characterful town offered plenty to stimulate a writer's imagination, from the narrow alleyways to the ruined abbey on the headland and the town's long association with the mourning stone jet, not to mention the North Sea crashing over the harbour walls in stormy weather. It was in Whitby that Stoker alighted on the name Dracula after research in the town's library, and many key pieces of the story originated here, including the eponymous blood-sucker coming ashore on a Russian vessel.

Day 2

On the far side of the bridge turn right and walk along beside the harbour past Whitby Fish Quay and the Dracula Experience. At the far end go round the hairpin and take the steps up on to the clifftop underneath the whalebone arch near the statue of Captain Cook. *Just along from the statue is a finger post sign*

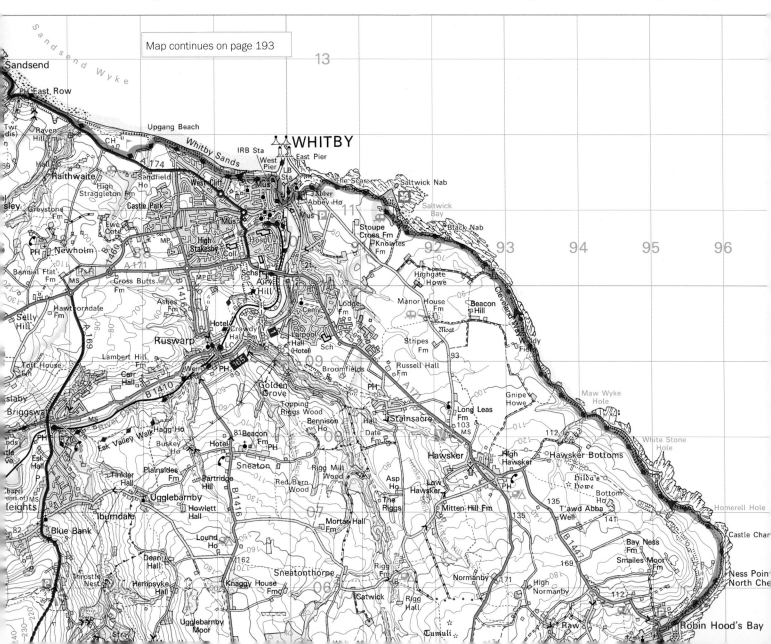

Map continues on page 193

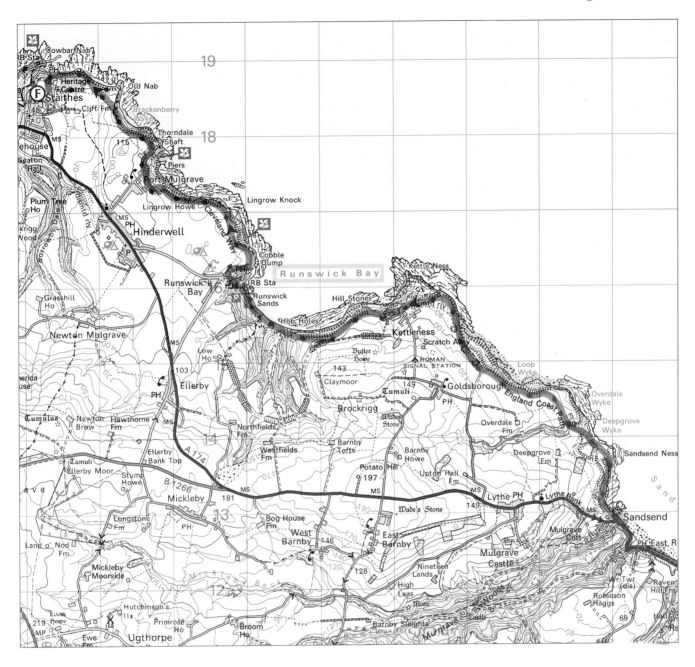

showing the destination and distance of Cook's voyages including Alaska 16,6990 miles (27,342km), New Zealand 12,090 miles (19,456km) and Tahiti 11,830 miles (19,038km).

Between Whitby and Sandsend the official route of the England Coast Path sets off on surfaced clifftop paths past houses, then turns left up a small valley to head inland around a golf course via the pavement of the A174. However, unless it's high tide or the weather is unfavourable, a more enjoyable option is to walk along the wide and sandy beach for 5km to **Sandsend**.

After the bustle of Whitby, Sandsend is a much more peaceful seaside location with handily placed cafés and shops. Follow the road to the far end and walk through the car park for steps up to a wide track. This former railway line allows good progress, but at the closed tunnel there's a particularly stiff staircase up to the cliffs above. The path now hugs the clifftop all the way to **Runswick Bay**, 8km from Sandsend, and there are ever more dramatic views along what is a high and, in places, eroding coastline.

The final descent to **Runswick Sands** is a bit of scramble across slippery rocks and bare earth. From here the route along the beach is occasionally impassable for a short period at high tide and signs advise walkers to wait for the waters to recede before continuing.

Walk up the steep pavement from the bay, following signs for a loop through woodland, then at the top continue along the road to the junction and turn right through the car park of a hotel. The field-edge route hugs the clifftop once more and takes to a lane through **Port Mulgrave** for a short while.

In the distance are the giant cliffs at Boulby, which at 203m are the highest on England's east coast. The path now drops down to finish at the delectable little fishing village of **Staithes**, partly hidden in a gap between the cliffs.

Voyages of discovery

The illustrious explorer and navigator James Cook began his career as a Merchant Navy apprentice in the 1740s, working out of Whitby on ships transporting coal. In 1755 he joined the navy and since Whitby was by now one of England's foremost ports and shipbuilding centres, Cook used his knowledge and experience to good effect to captain successive Whitby-built ships. He completed three epic voyages that took him to every continent, becoming the first person to sail around the world in both directions. His were truly scientific voyages of discovery, circumnavigating and charting New Zealand for the first time and debunking the commonly held belief of a Great Southern Continent in a temperate zone of the Southern Hemisphere. You can find out more at the Captain Cook Memorial Museum at Whitby and the heritage centre at the end of the walk called The Staithes Story.

▲   *The end of the walk at Staithes*   ▶   *Seaham Fleet Rock (photo: Chiz Dakin)*

Seaham to Hartlepool

Start	Seaham (Hall Beach car park) NZ 430 495
Finish	Hartlepool (The Headland) NZ 531 338
Distance	26km (16 miles)
Total ascent	545m (1790ft)
Time	6hr 30min
Terrain	Low cliffs, beaches and wooded denes, a few short slopes, mostly easy paths
Map	OS Explorer 308 Durham & Sunderland, 306 Middlesbrough & Hartlepool/OS Landranger 88 & 93
Refreshments	Numerous cafés and pubs in Seaham and Hartlepool, but nothing else on the actual route (nearest at Easington Colliery and Horden, 1.6km off route)
Public transport	Regular, fast and direct bus and train services between Seaham and Hartlepool
Parking	Car parks in Seaham, roadside at Hartlepool Headland

Map continues on page 198

This is a remarkable story about coastal regeneration and recovery. Less than 20 years ago, the County Durham shoreline between Seaham and Hartlepool was so disfigured by mining that the beaches were literally black from dumped coal spoil. It was pollution on a massive scale and ecosystems 6.4km out to sea were affected. Indeed, the landscape was so ghastly that it was used for scenes for a prison planet in the film *Alien 3*. Fast forward two decades and this Heritage Coast is once more a healthy, thriving natural environment and nearly all traces of what went before have disappeared. This is a shoreline re-born; and this long but straightforward walk along the top of the green, peaceful and wildlife-rich cliffs is now a real pleasure.

▲ *Blast Beach, Seaham (photo: Chiz Dakin)*

From the war memorial on Seaham seafront walk southwards past the harbour and marina and along the pavement to the car park at **Nose's Point**. Continue on the obvious clifftop path past the site of Dawdon Colliery, now completely vanished. At **Chourdon Point** you can continue for a there-and-back route down steep steps down to the rocky beach at Hawthorn Hive; otherwise head inland across the meadow and over the railway via a footbridge.

Turn left and follow the waymarked path as it drops down to cross the stream via a footbridge among the trees at **Hawthorn Dene**. After this, the route winds its way up the far side to go beneath the high-arched viaduct and resumes its clifftop progress (take the top path under the southernmost arch, not the first turning). *Hawthorn Dene is one of eight so-called denes along the Durham Heritage Coast, which are simply deep and narrow wooded valleys that run down to the sea.*

At **Shippersea Point**, 7km into the walk, the path veers away from the railway and approaching Easington Colliery it becomes surfaced for a while, then kinks inland to skirt **Fox Holes Dene**. Simply look for the waymarks and keep to the mostly obvious clifftop route. Nearing **Horden**, there are expansive views along the shoreline southwards and at the National Trust's **Warren House Gill** the path drops down to the beach, where you can appreciate for yourself how this once coal-blackened scene has been transformed.

From Horden Beach climb immediately back up on a steep and semi-overgrown flight of steps. On the clifftop there are seats, interpretation panels and an artwork remembering the former coal mine at this location which, like all the others, has given way to a re-profiled clifftop landscape of healthy grassland. *There's lots of creative public artwork along the walk, from the Tommy sculpture at Seaham through*

to Horden's Little Tern, *and the* Andy Capp *statue on The Headland at Hartlepool.*

Horden Colliery was sunk in 1900, mainly to work under-sea coal deposits. At its height it produced 4200 tons a day from its four seams and employed over 4000 men. The mine closed in 1987, leaving the mammoth task of re-landscaping 500,000 tons of spoil which, according to the excellent Heritage Coastal Footpath guide to the present-day path, had 'slumped over the cliffs onto the beach

below'. However, when the mine closed and the pumps were turned off, rising minewater also risked polluting local aquifers and potentially affecting drinking water, so a pioneering treatment scheme was developed that involves flowing the polluted water over aerating cascades to increase the amount of oxygen in the water. It is then allowed to settle in vast lagoons where the iron particles are safely removed and natural reedbeds help clean it further.

The coast path resumes its route along the low cliffs before turning left to join a tarmac lane down to the beach once more. Stay on the track as it bends around the foot of the low cliffs and crosses the wide and open mouth of **Castle Eden Dene**. This is just under the halfway point of the walk, roughly 11.3km from Seaham. On the far side of the valley mouth return to the broad clifftop, with the path running through a meadow of wild grasses and flowers.

The Durham Heritage Coast boasts a succession of **noteworthy nature reserves**, including the 6.4km long Castle Eden National Nature Reserve, famous for its semi-natural ash and wych elm woodland. Nearby is Blackhall Rocks, a local nature reserve managed by Durham Wildlife Trust, where rather unusually the Magnesian limestone which underlies the boulder clay comes to the surface. The thin soils and high lime content give rise to a very specific range of wildflowers and grasses, so that along the path in June and July you may see rock rose, common spotted orchids, gorse and bloody cranesbill, while skylarks trill overhead and buntings, pipits and short-eared owls are all present. Also look out for the rare Durham brown argus butterfly on sunny days.

There are more fine views along the coast from the path at **Blackhall Colliery**, especially southwards beyond Hartlepool

▲ *The coast near Horden (photo: Chiz Dakin)*

The coast approaching Hartlepool

towards the far-off North Yorkshire cliffs. The path detours around Blue House Gill and again kinks inland approaching a caravan park. As the railway line gets closer, go round the outer edge of a caravan site to reach the visitor car park at **Crimdon Park**.

Hartlepool is now in sight ahead, just under 7km away. Go through the car park and down to Crimdon Dunes, past the RSPB warden's hut where volunteers keep a summertime watch on nesting Little terns – stay out of the fenced enclosures and keep all dogs on leads.

From Crimdon Dunes follow coast path waymarks along a track across a golf course and then around its edge above the beach. However, if conditions allow, a walk along the firm foreshore of **North Sands** is possible until the promenade takes over and leads to **The Headland**, the historic part of **Hartlepool** overlooking the harbour, where the walk ends. *The Headland contains the impressive St Hilda's Church, a 16.5m lighthouse and a military museum called Heugh Battery which once defended the town from attack by the German Navy.*

Turning the Tide

At their peak the six coastal collieries, including Dawdon, Easington and Blackhall, employed many thousands of men and production was on a massive scale. The huge output of coal broke national and even European records and Easington Colliery stretched 8km out under the sea. But for a century the spoil was simply tipped over the cliffs, turning the beaches black, and it only stopped in the early 1990s when the mines all closed. Since then a £10 million reclamation project called Turning the Tide has attempted to reverse the environmental damage; but nature has also proved a healer. Through wave action the beaches have been naturally cleansed, the seawater is now much clearer and so seaweed and other underwater vegetation has begun to grow again. Slowly the food chain has re-established itself, from worms and shellfish through to fish and birds. There are still some dark traces on a few of the beaches, but the transformation is remarkable. For more on this story go to www.durhamheritagecoast.org.

▲ *Picking coal off the beach at Easington Colliery in the 1970s (photo: Mike Jones)* ▶ *Bamburgh Castle*

Walk 30
Craster to Bamburgh

Start	Craster (harbour) NU 257 199
Finish	Bamburgh NU 180 349
Distance	22km (13.7 miles)
Total ascent	110m (360ft)
Time	5hr
Terrain	Low cliffs, rocky foreshore, beach and dune paths
Map	OS Explorer 332 & 340/OS Landranger 113
Refreshments	Cafés or pubs in Craster, Low Newton, Beadnell, Seahouses and Bamburgh, in particular the Shoreline Café at Craster and Copper Kettle Café at Bamburgh
Public transport	Regular daily bus service between Craster, Seahouses, Beadnell and Bamburgh
Parking	Car parks at Craster and Bamburgh (charge)

Away from Newcastle's urban hinterland, Northumberland's quiet coastline is characterised by dunes and yawning sandy bays. It's an open and mostly undeveloped landscape, a glorious place to walk, although it can be a little bracing if a keen onshore wind is blowing. A particularly eye-catching feature is a succession of castles and this route visits one ruined and another restored, finishing with far-off views of a third. Depending on the weather conditions and state of the tide there are numerous opportunities to walk long sections of beach and foreshore; and a good daily bus service, with options to shorten the route at Beadnell and Seahouses, makes this an ideal walk to complete using public transport.

Map continues on page 205

From Craster's diminutive harbour follow the sign for **Dunstanburgh Castle** northwards past a row of cottages and out across the low and open grassy cliffs. The ruined castle, which is already in sight, occupies a prominent clifftop position and you can go inside to explore the twin-towered keep and battlements (charge).

Don't be alarmed if you're assailed by drifting smoke during your walk around Craster. It's very likely to be emanating from the **smokehouse run by L. Robson & Sons** who, for over a century, have been producing tasty kippers smoked in the traditional way. Kippers are herring, which are then split, soaked and hung on tenterhooks over smouldering whitewood shavings and oak sawdust for up to 16 hours. Delicious! The Smokehouse Shop is open daily for purchases, although whether you want to walk a full day in the sun with a pair of aromatic kippers in your rucksack is questionable. Fortunately they also have an online shop at www.kipper.co.uk where they also sell smoked salmon and haddock.

▲ *Ruins of Dunstanburgh Castle*

Drop down to the left of the castle and follow the well-walked path through the dunes beside a golf course and on around **Embleton Bay**. As with so much of this walk, there's an obvious and easy path through the dunes; or, if conditions allow, simply walk along the sandy beach. The rocky foreshore quickly gives way to a crescent of unblemished sand lapped by the cold, dark waves of the North Sea. As you get further on

make sure to look over your right shoulder, since the elevated battlements of Dunstanburgh framed by the simple, natural beauty of Embleton Bay provide one of the iconic sights on the Northumberland coast.

At **Low Newton-by-the-Sea** (toilets) there is a well-preserved square of traditional fishing cottages, which includes the Ship Inn. Join a path, signposted Beadnell, across the

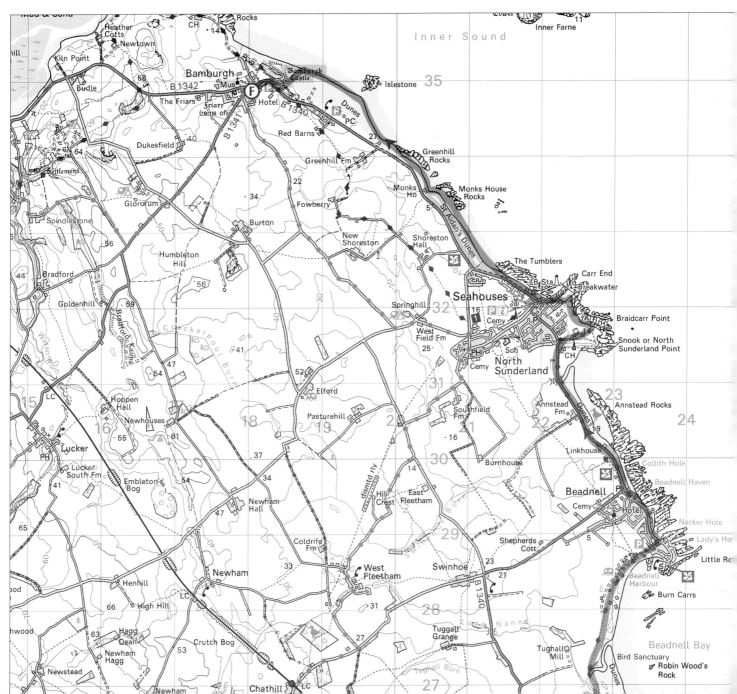

Dunstanburgh Castle at dawn (photo: Chiz Dakin)

low headland of **Newton Point**. *You will see waymarks for St Oswald's Way, a 156km walking trail from Holy Island to near Hexham that visits places associated with Northumberland's 7th-century king.*

Now **Beadnell Bay** opens up and although it's tempting to return to the sand the more direct route is along the path through the dunes, via Newton Steads car park and across **Newton Links**. This is also advisable because further on you are asked to avoid a sensitive area of beach beside Long Nanny burn used by nesting birds between May and July.

Each summer for the past few decades National Trust rangers and volunteers have roped off a small area of beach on Beadnell Bay to allow **Arctic terns** to nest (there are also a few pairs of Little terns and ringed plovers). The slender seabird has the longest migration route of any in the world, flying from Antarctica to get here, but in 2020 the terns failed to fledge any chicks for the first time in 40 years. A combination of storm damage, predation by rats and stoats (when COVID restrictions meant volunteers were unable to patrol the site), and disturbance by recreational users disrupted the usual nesting arrangements. It's hoped that the terns will recover in future years, but please keep dogs on a

lead, observe local signs and admire these handsome and intrepid birds from a distance.

On the far side of the wooden footbridge that spans **Long Nanny burn** follow the coast path across Tughall Mill Links and via a caravan park to emerge in **Beadnell**, which at 12km from Craster is just over the half way point of the walk.

Walk ahead through the village to the coast road and head north towards Seahouses. Drop down for a beach walk if conditions allow, otherwise follow the path through the narrow Annstead Links behind the dunes. If you choose the former, at the far end of the sand by a low line of red cliffs climb steps for a public footpath across the golf course to the road. Turn right and right again for a signposted path back out across the fairways to the clifftop and the short walk into the small but popular and well-equipped resort of **Seahouses**.

On the quay at Seahouses harbour there are several kiosks where you can book boat trips to the **Farne Islands**, around 4km offshore. There are 28 separate islands, although many are so small that they disappear at high tide, but in the 7th century the largest was the base for the solitary St Cuthbert. Today the Farne Islands are managed by the

National Trust and better known as the home of around 100,000 pairs of nesting seabirds, as well as a colony of grey seals. May to July is the main bird-breeding season and you can land in carefully controlled visits. The sight and sound of so many birds so close up on both the water and on land is terrific, with up to 23 species including tern, puffin, eider, shag, guillemot and razorbill.

Go past the harbour and up the ramp beside the lifeboat station to turn right on the coast road towards Bamburgh. A path soon drops down to the beach; and although the formal route of the England Coast Path is through **St Aidan's Dunes**,

if conditions allow a far more attractive option is simply to walk the beach all the way to Bamburgh (about 4km). At low tide there is a wide and continuous strip of firm sand and occasional rocky shelves, providing a stirring end to the walk as the mighty fortress of Bamburgh Castle draws nearer. *The dark platforms are a dolerite rock known locally as whinstone, which also underpins Bamburgh Castle and the Farne Islands and forms the Whin Sill geological feature across northern England.*

Just before you reach **Bamburgh Castle** follow a sandy path through the dunes to access the castle car park and from there into the centre of the village.

A coast of castles

Northumberland's castles each have a fascinating backstory. At one extreme is Alnwick, which despite 950 years of history is perhaps better known as Hogwarts in the first two Harry Potter films. Then there's Warkworth, where the rebellious Harry Hostpur and the Percy family had their base. On the coast is Dunstanburgh Castle, started in 1313 by a powerful baron in opposition to the king, but after a siege by Yorkist forces in the Wars of the Roses it decayed to the present-day ruins. The formidable defences of Bamburgh Castle, sitting high above the village, replaced an early Celtic fort and then a Norman castle, so that most of what you see today dates from a more modern restoration. In sight further north is Lindisfarne Castle, which in fact is more Edwardian country house than military fortification, although Holy Island is of course better known as the base of Celtic Christianity and St Aidan's 7th-century monastery.

Beach north of Seahouses

Useful websites

General information

Official England Coast Path site
www.nationaltrail.co.uk/en_GB/trails/england-coast-path

Natural England
www.gov.uk/government/publications/
england-coast-path-overview-of-progress

English Heritage
www.english-heritage.org.uk

Long Distance Walkers' Association
www.ldwa.org.uk

National authority for lighthouses
www.trinityhouse.co.uk

National Coastwatch Institution
www.nci.org.uk

National parks
www.nationalparks.uk

National Trust
www.nationaltrust.org.uk/coast-and-beaches

Quintin Lake's coastal photography project
www.theperimeter.uk

The Ramblers
www.ramblers.org.uk/EnglandCoastPath

Royal National Lifeboat Institution
www.rnli.org

South West Coast Path Association
www.southwestcoastpath.org.uk

UK Beach Guide
www.thebeachguide.co.uk

Environment and wildlife

Areas of Outstanding Natural Beauty
www.landscapesforlife.org.uk

Marine Conservation Society
www.mcsuk.org

Royal Society for the Protection of Birds
www.rspb.org.uk

Surfers Against Sewage
www.sas.org.uk

The Wildlife Trusts
www.wildlifetrusts.org

Tourist information

Public transport
www.traveline.info

www.bbc.co.uk/weather

www.tidetimes.org.uk

www.metoffice.gov.uk/weather/specialist-forecasts/
coast-and-sea/beach-forecast-and-tide-times